Wait Wait...I'm Not Done Yet!

Wait Wait...I'm Not Done Yet!

by

Carl Kasell

with special memories from

Bob Edwards • Susan Stamberg
Cokie Roberts • Nina Totenberg • Jean Cochran
Paula Poundstone • Mo Rocca • Roy Blount, Jr.
Tom Bodett • Amy Dickinson • Roxanne Roberts
and many others

Foreword by Peter Sagal

BANTRY BAY PUBLISHING
CHICAGO

Wait Wait...I'm Not Done Yet!
by Carl Kasell
© 2014
All rights reserved.
No part of this publication may be reproduced, stored in a retrieval
system or transmitted in any form or by any means without the prior
written permission of the publisher.

Correspondence to the publisher should be by e-mail:
bantrybaypublishing@gmail.com
www.bantrybaybooks.com

Printed in the United States of America
at Lake Book Manufacturing, Melrose Park, Illinois

ISBN 978-0-9850673-4-2

Library of Congress Cataloging-Publication Data has been applied for.

Front cover photo: Tony Nagelmann / NPR
Back cover "rapper" photo: Nelson Hsu/NPR
Back flap photo of Carl: Melody Kramer
Illustrations on pages 158 and 178 by Elizabeth Brandt for NPR
Background photo on Page 240 by Phil Hauck

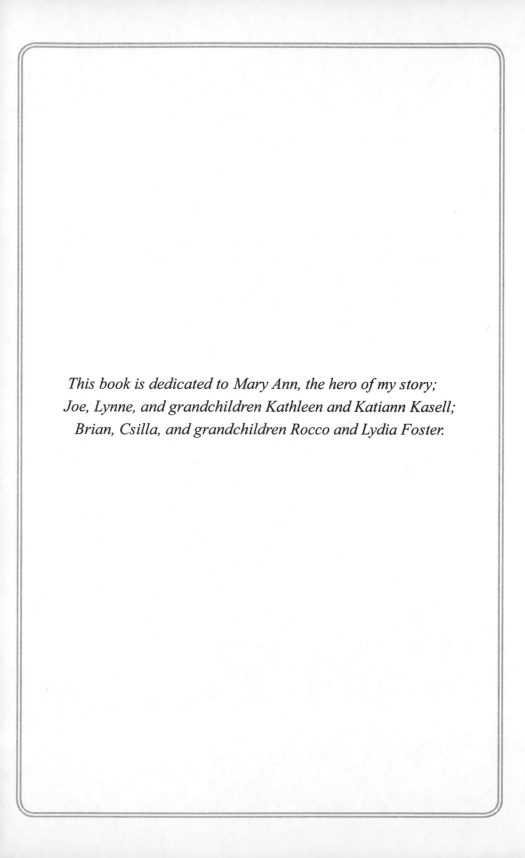

*This book is dedicated to Mary Ann, the hero of my story;
Joe, Lynne, and grandchildren Kathleen and Katiann Kasell;
Brian, Csilla, and grandchildren Rocco and Lydia Foster.*

©Jerry A. Schulman

Wait Wait...I'm Not Done Yet!

contents

Introduction   xi
Foreword   xv

ONE   Goldsboro, North Carolina   19
             Jackie Kasell (brother) memories   27
             Mary Kasell Groce (sister) memories   31
TWO   Hooked at an Early Age   35
THREE   Sacramento!   51
             Joe Kasell (son) memories   63
FOUR   Now Pitching, Carl Kasell!   69
FIVE   Elvis and Katie Couric   79
SIX   Meeting Mary Ann   87
             Brian Foster (stepson) memories   103
SEVEN   Morning Edition   109
             Bob Edwards memories   129
             Nina Totenberg memories   133
             Jean Cochran memories   135
             Cokie Roberts memories   141
             Jay Kernis memories   143
             Susan Stamberg memories   144
EIGHT   Radio From Downtown   147
NINE   Wait Wait...Don't Tell Me!   157
             Paula Poundstone memories   183
             Mo Rocca memories   187

Roxanne Roberts memories   189

Adam Felber memories   193

Roy Blount, Jr. memories   197

Amy Dickinson memories   199

Brian Babylon memories   203

Faith Salie memories   207

Tom Bodett memories   210

Margaret Low Smith memories   211

TEN   Magic Edition   213

ELEVEN   Kennedy Center Honors   221

TWELVE   North Carolina   225

THIRTEEN   Howard Stern   229

So long, suckers!   231

President Barack Obama   233

Stephen Colbert   235

Katie Couric   237

Acknowledgments   239

introduction

As I sit here in my "office for life" at NPR in Washington, DC, I often think about what a good time I've had and what good people I've worked with, both here and, before that, at radio stations in North Carolina and Virginia.

The radio bug bit me early. When I was in first grade, our class did a Christmas program that aired on WGBR, our local station in Goldsboro, North Carolina. I sang a song. That launched my career.

Radio turned me into a creature of habit. For 30 years, I lived by the clock. I arrived at NPR at 2 a.m. and began putting together my newscasts, which had to be timed out exactly to eight minutes, 30 seconds. They consisted of a three-minute first section, a two-minute second section, and finally a three-and-a-half minute section that typically contained business stories. For most of those years, I started reading newscasts at exactly 5:01 a.m. and continued doing so at the top of each hour through 11 o'clock.

Every morning at 10:30 a.m., I would sit at my desk and peel a banana, a tradition that may date back to my mother's banana pudding. Nobody made banana pudding like my mother. Nobody. I can still taste it and I miss it, and I miss her. So much of who I am, and the person you hear on the radio, is because of the values instilled by my mother and father, and by the traditions that came with being a North Carolinian.

Countless other people mentioned in this book have had an impact on my life: people you've heard of like Andy Griffith and Charles Kuralt, and many more people you've probably not heard of, such as Clifton Britton and Vassie Balkcum.

While my newscasts seemed to the listener to be solo performances, I was part of a team of talented journalists, producers, directors, editors and others necessary to run an organization like NPR, and a program like *Wait Wait...Don't Tell Me!* In these pages, you'll read about many of them. Many others, like Bob Edwards, Susan Stamberg, Cokie Roberts, Nina Totenberg, Jean Cochran, Peter Sagal, Paula Poundstone, Mo Rocca, Roxanne Roberts, Doug Berman and others will share their memories of our time together.

Any number of people told me over the last 10 or so years that I should write a memoir. I didn't give it much thought because I didn't have time. Thirty years of anchoring *Morning Edition* and, for an overlapping 11 years doing *Wait Wait...Don't Tell Me!,* and for one year, also hosting *Early Morning Edition*, kept me plenty busy.

After I retired from doing the news in 2009, I gave a little more thought to the suggestions of a book, but got no further than that. But in the months since I retired from *Wait Wait,* I found enough time on my hands that writing a book seemed like a worthwhile project.

There are three reasons for this book that go hand in hand. While I'm creating a record of my life that my grandchildren and their children can read and get an idea of who I was and how I spent my life, it's also a way to pull back the NPR curtain a little as an expression of my gratitude to the wonderful listeners who have made it all so rewarding.

Also, it's a way to thank the remarkable people I've had the pleasure of working with over my 60 years on the air. My colleagues gave me the best that they had. They were excellent at what they did, so easy to work with, and it was such a pleasure being associated with these people. I have great affection for them and whenever I see them, I walk up to them and give them a hug. We worked hard together to make NPR what it is today. It's a darn good network.

When I think back on all of the big stories that I reported on as a news anchor, it's as if I had a front-row seat on the world. Knowing that mine was often the first voice millions of listeners heard when historic events were unfolding was an honor and privilege. Alistair Cooke, the legendary British journalist and television personality, once told a story about a little girl who loved radio. He asked her why, and she said, "Because the pictures are better." In my first radio class in high school, I was taught to create theater of the mind where listeners would use my words to create their own images. That's the beauty and power of radio when it's done well.

My favorite time at NPR was as official scorekeeper and judge for *Wait Wait...Don't Tell Me!* Taping those shows before audiences at the Chase Bank Auditorium in Chicago and on the road in many wonderful venues, was loads of fun and gave me a chance to meet the listeners that I felt I had known and talked to for so many years. And it gave me the opportunity to be someone that I couldn't be as a newscaster. Peter Sagal has described me as: "Pure, Grade A, North Carolina ham." We had a great team, and while we were the ones reading the scripts and telling the jokes, there are many people behind the scenes who work so hard. When I see, and hear, how well *Wait Wait* is doing, it makes me feel good knowing that I was there at the beginning.

As you'll read, I have long been fascinated by magic, which was another outlet for the "ham" in me. I was lucky to connect with NPR producer and director Barry Gordemer, who is a terrific magician, puppeteer and puppet maker, and a great friend. We formed a magic show called "Magic Edition," and among our amazing feats, we sawed one of NPR's most famous personalities in half.

When you get to be a certain age, people start asking when you're going to retire. My answer is always the same, and I borrowed it from the Smothers Brothers. About 10 years ago in Boston I was on a program with them and when I told Dick I thought they'd have retired by now, he said, "Retire is what people do from work. I don't call this work." That's just how I feel. I am the luckiest man around to be able to have made a living doing something I love for so many years. It's truly been a joy for me and I've loved every minute of it.

Even though I go to my office at NPR nearly every day and record voice mail messages for *Wait Wait* winners, I still have a lot of time on my hands. Maybe Barry and I should get our magic act together again. Or, as I've told my friends Stephen Colbert and Katie Couric: "As you go forward and need an announcer, I'm your guy." I'm not done yet.

— Carl Kasell

foreword

Presumably, the day I was born was the most important day of my life, but I don't remember that. I do remember the day I met Carl Kasell, though, so that tops my personal list.

Carl and I had been working together for at least six months as we rehearsed and then performed the very first *Wait Wait* shows, but we hadn't yet met. You see, when the show first started, everyone recorded remotely. I was a panelist based in New York who eventually stumbled into becoming the host based in Chicago, and Carl had to stay in Washington, DC, to keep giving you people the news. Wisely, you folks didn't trust anyone else.

So it wasn't until June 1998, at that year's Public Radio Convention, that I finally shook the hand of the man who was then, and has been since, my true better half.

I remember Carl's warm smile and kind eyes as he said, "Peter Sagal, it's so nice to meet you," and continued to shake my hand. I was entranced by the sound of my name — my own name! — as enunciated by that, the most famous and welcome of all voices. It's been 16 years since then, and I still thrill whenever I hear it.

Right away, I knew that Carl had far more up his sleeve than his inimitable gravitas and the random playing cards he keeps there for his magic tricks (if you ever want to know true joy, ask Carl to do magic for you). Unknown to almost everyone up to that time, Carl was more than just a natural newscaster, he was a born showman, who used to do theater back in the day. He was lying in wait, biding his time, just itching for the right opportunity to show the world his panoply of skills.

The next time we met was in Washington, DC, where we had been flown to shoot some publicity stills. Standing around in a performance studio, posing for some dull shots of us in our sport jackets, Carl spied a grand piano in the corner. Soon, he was lying on top of it, chin in hand, looking like a more dapper Michelle Pfeiffer from *The Fabulous Baker Boys*, while I pretended to play the piano. He batted his eyes at me and said, "I've always wanted to do this."

NPR

In the years since, Carl and I have traveled around the country, doing shows in places ranging from half-filled concrete civic auditoriums to Carnegie Hall. We did countless shows in our studios and our home theater in Chicago, not to mention all the recep-

NPR

Peter Sagal and Carl Kasell with their
traditional pre-show hand clasp

tions, parties, fundraisers and taping sessions. And through them all, Carl showed himself to be the greatest collaborator ever — one who never demands the spotlight, but just seems to draw it to himself naturally.

Carl has put up with endless travel, silly jokes, countless assaults on his dignity, and my stumbling and stuttering away through shows right next to him, and all he ever has to say about it is, "I can't complain." He actually can't! After one of our tapings I challenged him to do it. I said, "Go ahead, Carl, you have a pass: Complain. Whine. Piss and moan about something. Nobody will hold it against you."

And Carl thought for a minute, he hemmed and hawed — it was the first time I ever saw him at a loss for words — and then he looked thoughtful and said, "You know, I really enjoy just about everything I do." And Carl has done a lot in his 60-plus years of broadcasting, much of it documented in the following pages.

As Scorekeeper Emeritus, Carl remains public radio's most dashing and beloved personality and we will miss him and his famously understated wit. As we began taping Carl's final show in Chicago, I said, "Carl, we thought that the best tribute to you would be to just do a really good show."

He replied, "Well, it would be about time."

— Peter Sagal, host of *Wait Wait...Don't Tell Me!*

— one —

goldsboro, north carolina

April 2, 1934 is when I made my entrance. I was the first of four children Eddie Kasell and Lela Mitchell Kasell would love and care for. In the coming years, sisters Grace and Mary, and a brother, Jackie, joined us. Our parents were wonderful, hardworking people who gave us a good home, although I know it wasn't always easy. We didn't have much. Our mother was a Mitchell, and her parents died before I was born. As the story goes, at one time her father was a wealthy farmer, but the family fell on hard times.

My mother, Lela Mitchell, back row on the right, with her brother, sister, father and step-mother in the late 1920s

Our grandparents on my dad's side lived with us in Goldsboro until they passed away. Kasell is of German heritage; in fact, there's a city in Germany called Kassell, but various efforts to trace our roots ended in the mid-1800s in South Carolina.

My father was not a formally educated man. Mother, herself unable to finish high school, taught him how to read. Sometimes it was challenging for him to get good work. He did manual labor, working in a sawmill and a box factory. Then, shortly after Pearl Harbor, the War Department ordered an airstrip on the southern out-

19

My father, Eddie Kasell, and mother, Lela Mitchell Kasell, circa 1929

skirts of Goldsboro be activated as an Army Air Corps training base. In 1942, it was dedicated as Seymour Johnson Air Force Base. Seymour was a local boy who joined the Navy and was killed in a training flight in 1941. It is the only Air Force base named in honor of a naval officer, and it became the home of the 326th Fighter Group. The base's primary mission was to train P-47 fighter pilots, which provided a great deal of entertainment for me. We lived nearby, and I could see the planes flying in and out, day and night. It was so exciting sitting on our porch and watching the planes dogfighting as part of their training. Throughout the war, those pilots were among the first and most frequent to fly bombing runs inside Germany.

The famed P-47 fighter-bombers on the tarmac at Seymour Johnson AFB in Goldsboro

Photo courtesy Dale Genius, Director and Curator, Louisiana History Museum

Since we didn't have much, it didn't take much to entertain us. Dad had a rattletrap of a car that he tore the rumble seat out of. He built up the back to make a flatbed where he could haul things. That's where we kids would sit. We'd take a nice ride and maybe stop for ice cream. There were big, wide fenders over the front wheels, and sometimes Dad let us sit on the fenders. We'd hang on, and away we went. What a ride! He was very careful with us so we didn't fall off, and I'm sure we didn't go more than a few miles per hour, but it seemed like we were going fast. That sure was fun.

The air base is where Dad came in contact with German POWs. As many as 500 were housed at Seymour Johnson, and because so many of our farm boys were off fighting the war, the Germans were put to work raising crops and harvesting timber. I remember my father telling us he'd made friends with many of the POWs and that they told him that they loved America so much, when the war was over they wanted to come back, build a home and live here. Although they were the enemy, they were treated fairly by the military and the community. The Germans who worked in the kitchen liked my dad and the familiar Kasell name. They would slip him things that most people in town didn't have access to, like lard, flour and sugar. Mom would use them for cooking and baking, and sugar also had another use: Dad used it to pay doctor bills.

Dad and Mom told us that the POWs were just like us, human beings caught up in the war. There was this feeling about the Germans that someday we would all live together peacefully.

Until then, our parents decided that our name was a liability, so we changed the pronunciation of Kasell to "kuh-SELL" to avoid any connection to that town in Germany. I continued pronouncing it that way after the war until 1950, my sophomore year in high school. My radio class teacher said he didn't care what I called myself outside

On the air in 1948 as Carl "kuh-SELL"

of radio, but it was important that I pronounced my name "Castle," because it sounded better and was easier to understand and remember.

This may seem odd coming from someone my age, but I miss my parents a lot. They were wonderful, and we had a good, loving family. My mom was just the best. "Anything for my boy!" she would often say. Mom was a great cook and had a green thumb, with a big garden where she raised much of what we ate. She knew exactly what to plant and how to plant them. Mother grew butter beans, peas, tomatoes and a variety of vegetables, and she'd mostly grow them for canning purposes. She'd take tomatoes, boil and slice them, put them in a jar, seal the top and we'd have tomatoes all winter. She was a wonderful seamstress, making and mending nearly all

Mom and Dad on their 50th wedding anniversary, December 12, 1981

of our clothes. I remember her and the women in the neighborhood getting together at night for noisy quilting parties, gossiping as they pulled all those remnants together into a beautiful quilt. Dad built a large bracket for the ladies to stretch their quilts over as they made them.

Dad was handy in that way. He was not a carpenter, but you'd think he was. We lived in a rented house with a large yard, and he built a chicken coop where we raised chickens for food and eggs. I thought it was nice that he built a shelf of nesting boxes where the hens could lay their eggs in straw. We didn't have running water, so dad built a wooden gutter and trough system along the roof of the house. When a thunderstorm would come up, the rainwater ran down the trough into wash tubs. We used the water to wash clothes. Dad was good at analyzing problems, figuring out solutions and building things, a very inventive guy. That is a quality my brother Jackie inherited.

As a boy, Jackie took all his toys apart, always curious about how things worked. As an adult, he got into the medical business, eventually specializing in creating devices for patients experiencing arrhythmia. It used to be that doctors would open up the heart and make an incision to remedy the irregular heartbeats, but Jackie was involved in creating a catheter that's inserted into the leg and runs up through an artery into the heart and delivers a jolt of electricity. When I visited him at Duke University Medical Center, a doctor described for me what I was seeing on a monitor as the procedure was being done. He said, "You see how that works?"

"Yes."

"Your brother did that."

A bit of irony: I was diagnosed with an irregular heartbeat several years ago, but it wasn't so severe that I needed Jackie's procedure. My doctor switched me to decaf coffee, and that took care of it.

Jackie currently spends a lot of time in Florida. I always ask him, "Jackie, why are you down there?"

"It's warm, Carl."

Jackie is such a likeable guy, and I love my brother very much.

Here we are, the Kasell kids: me, Grace, Jackie and Mary

My sister, Grace Kasell Newber, became a brilliant organizer of offices and organizations in Wilmington, North Carolina, and was quite successful. We were devastated when she was killed in a car accident in 2011. Grace was a sweet person with a smile for everyone.

My baby sister, Mary Kasell Groce, still resides in Goldsboro, where she retired as a banking officer from BB & T, buying and selling mortgages. Mary also was invited to teach real estate finance at Wayne Community College.

When I was in first or second grade, I missed a lot of school. I was what was known back then as a "sickly kid." Today, they might give you a pill and send you back to school, but back then, I'd spend a week or so at home sometimes. I loved to read and my teacher would drop off books for me. I couldn't get enough of them and spent a lot of time in the school and public libraries. That love of reading was important to my broadcasting career. I always tell young people who want to get into the business that to be good broadcasters, they need to be good writers, and to be good writers, they need to read and read and read.

My brother Carl was a great big brother, but he was a tough act to follow. He is four-and-a-half years older and was always one of the top students, well-liked by everyone. When I got to school, the teachers expected me to be like him. I wasn't, not even close, even though he helped me with my homework. I was a little wild growing up, Carl wasn't. He was smart, articulate, bookish, and I was convinced he had a photographic memory. Carl could sit down and read a document, and that was it; he knew it.

Goldsboro was a friendly place and small enough that everyone knew each other. We had a neighborhood full of kids and I was always out playing and riding my bike. But as far back as I can remember, Carl was always focused on being on the radio. And to be on the radio in a small town like that was the greatest thing in the world at that time. People admired Carl.

As a family, we got along very well. Our dad was the nicest person you'd ever want to meet. He was a hard worker, but Goldsboro was a difficult place to get a job in those days. It was especially hard for Dad because of his lack of education, but he was a talented fix-it man and liked to build things. That helped him get a job at the air base. When Pearl Harbor was bombed, I was only about three years old, but I remember how we were all listening to the radio and hearing the reports. There were many blackouts during the war and I can recall the lights in the city being turned off. One big thrill was

The Kasell brothers around 1945 on what looks to have been a cold day in Golds-boro, probably the beginning of Jackie's desire to be in Florida during the winters

when Dad took me out to the air base to see the planes up close.

Dad was a family person and was greatly influenced by his mother, my Grandmother Ida. She and Grandpa Eugene Kasell lived with us for many years until they died, and Grandma ruled the roost, or sure tried to. It didn't always go over well. My mother told me years later that Grandmother Ida spanked me one day when I was little, and my mother told her if she ever caught her spanking me again, she would spank Ida!

Mother was a total angel and you couldn't ask for a better person. She just knew how to handle people. She and Dad lived into their mid-80s and died within two years of each other. Dad was very active until he had a heart attack and died. Our mother lived to be 85 and it was a difficult death. She had just returned from a trip to visit Carl and didn't feel well. Mother went to the emergency room and as she was lying on the table, it was as though all the lights went out. She went blind and never regained her sight. Mother died in December and Carl's first wife, Clara, died a short time later.

We all loved Clara and I had grown very close to her as she and Carl lived with us for a while after they married. That period when the two women who meant the most to Carl died was tough on all of us, but especially on him. He went through so much heartache. I am so happy that Mary Ann came into Carl's life.

I'm very proud of Carl and all that he's accomplished, but I egg him on all the time, teasing him about being so famous. We all turned out okay, though. As Carl mentioned, I must have inherited Dad's gene for figuring things out and fixing them, and I also hit the top in my field. I had a research associate position at Duke and when physicians came up with a problem, it was my job to develop and design solutions. I was playing tennis one time and a few security police came looking for me because there was a doctor in DC who needed my advice about a cardiac patient. The job was challenging and rewarding, but overall, kind of funny because they basically gave me an honorary degree to get me out of high school.

To be able to turn the radio on anywhere in the United States and hear Carl? Wow. We get together when we can, but if it's in the winter, he has to come to Florida.

memories from
mary kasell groce

I didn't like *Wait Wait* at first. I knew other people did, including younger people. A friend told me that at UNC-Chapel Hill, there was a fan club of students who would have *Wait Wait* listening parties. But I didn't really get it until Carl arranged for us to attend a taping. I became a big fan after that!

Our family didn't have much growing up and I marvel at how our mother put things together, especially given that she had a privileged upbringing. After her mother died young, she had to learn to do everything around the house. She learned well and served us three big meals a day, starting with biscuits and grits for breakfast. Then it was off to work at a clothing store where she was a seamstress. At noon, she would come home to prepare lunch, even after our father retired. Then, at the end of the workday, she'd return home and prepare a big meal for all of us. She became a great baker, too, and could roll pastry out on the counter and it would roll out like silk. I still have the wooden bowl that she used to make biscuits and it's worn from her hands. The one thing our mother gave all of us was a great work ethic.

Carl is nine years older than me, and when I left for school in the morning, he would already be gone to work at the local radio station. He then left for college and went into the army before I was even in high school, so we were sister and brother, but we grew up in different eras.

Although Carl was a bit elusive as my brother, he was well known in town, always a leader and respected. I do remember being compared to Carl and people saying, your brother did this, why can't you?

Our father had a terrific sense of humor and Carl got some of his humor from him, and I suppose we all got some of that, as well as the kind, loving example that our parents set for us. They loved each other deeply and when our mother was in declining health, I took on many of the responsibilities of caring for her. She and I were listening to music one day and she said, "You don't know this, but when you children were not in the house, your daddy and I would turn on the Victrola and we would dance in the hallway."

My mother loved to dress up and it was important to her that we were dressed well, too. And she was quite a clotheshorse. When she passed away, I counted more than 60 pairs of shoes in her closet! She wore size five and a half, which was the size of the sample shoes from her clothing store.

We're very proud of Carl and his success, but other people seemed much more impressed with him than we were. I always get somebody saying excitedly, "I didn't know Carl was your brother!" It was just normal for us, and we accepted the success as part of his life. He was blessed with a wonderful voice, and he knew how to use it. Carl worked very hard for so long, and retirement will be interesting for him. We're so appreciative of Mary Ann and I'm so pleased that they seem so happy together.

Here's a little insight into what a great brother he has been: Carl has never forgotten my birthday. I always get flowers from Carl on my birthday. So did Grace before she died.

The shadow in the lower left corner is likely our mother's as she is taking a photo of her kids before Mary was born. That's Grace on the left, Jackie in the middle, and me, stylishly attired in some sort of mid-calf pants.

An aspiring broadcaster, around age six

hooked at an early age

My mom used to have to drag me out of the house to go play with other kids because I couldn't get enough of the radio. I was thrilled by what came out of that box, and I'd sit spellbound for hours if she would let me, listening to *The Lone Ranger, The House of Mystery, Superman, Batman* and on and on, one right after another. We had one of those large radio consoles, a furniture piece, and a potted plant behind it. Sometimes I would hide behind them and, with the radio turned off, pretend I was on the air and try to fool anyone who came by. I'm fairly certain I didn't.

My grandmother had a Victrola with the big 78 rpm records, and I would play disc jockey, talking in between songs. I'd tell jokes, give the time and temperature, make up commercials, just like the guy on the radio did. I fell in love with radio. Dad could see how taken I was with it, and he bought me a small table radio so I could listen to programs as I went to bed at night.

On weekends, Dad would take me to the local radio station, which was just off the highway outside of town. The doors weren't locked, so I could just walk in and look through the studio windows and watch the guys playing records and talking on the radio. I thought that was really cool, but even cooler was the teletype machine in a little room off to the side, just banging away as it typed all of the latest news. I thought that was fascinating and wished I could have had one at home.

One day I was walking down a street in Goldsboro and heard a familiar voice. I turned in the direction of the voice. The face wasn't familiar, but then I realized it was one of the voices I'd heard on the radio so many times. My gosh, so that's what he looks like! I'm sure there've been many listeners of mine over the years who said the same thing. I hope they weren't disappointed.

Fortune was on my side when I went to high school. Goldsboro High had an excellent drama department, one of the biggest in the South at that time, and the department offered a radio class. Of course, I took that class, and we had the opportunity to present a weekly student show that aired on the local station. We were taught how to create images using voice, sounds and music. I became active in the drama department and loved every minute of it.

I was also old enough to work and had an after-school job bagging groceries. My family depended on my help, both monetarily and for food. Once in a while I would get wrapped up in what I was doing in the radio class and would be late arriving at work. My dad heard about that and made it clear that the family came first. "Don't waste your time with that radio junk!" he said. "We need your help, Son." I had no desire to work at a grocery store my whole life, but I knew I had a responsibility to my family. Dad and Mom were products of the Depression and grew up with that work ethic. They passed on those same values but also made sure that we had it much easier than they did as children. I learned how to balance my wants and needs and found time for both the radio class and the grocery job.

My mother was very supportive, too, and I knew they were very proud of me as my career progressed. Before they died in their 80s, they enjoyed listening to me on the local station in North Carolina and, later, doing the morning news from Washington DC.

When it came to the many other people who had an influence on my career, let's begin with our high school drama and music teacher: Mr. Andrew Griffith. That's how he was formally listed in the Goldsboro High School yearbook, but the world would know him years later as the wise Sheriff Andy Taylor. It was his first job out of college, and he taught there from 1949-1952.

ANDREW GRIFFITH
Music, Dramatics

Years later, Andy had fun telling the story about his first day on the job at Goldsboro High, where he, with his impossibly thick, country-southern accent, was assigned a speech class. He was to teach students how to speak without an accent. "Talk about the blind leading the blind," he said. Things got worse when he decided to start off with the word "coffee." As he wrote it on the blackboard, he misspelled it. I never had Andy for a class, but I worked with him in other areas and he was a huge help to me, personally and professionally. What a guy he was!

During the summers for several years, he had a job at a show on the Outer Banks called *The Lost Colony,* which has gone on to become one of the longest-running plays in the country. It has been performed since 1937 in an outdoor amphitheater located on Roanoke Island at the site of Sir Walter Raleigh's original colony. Andy played Sir Walter and, for a time, I played Chief Wanchese, one of two Indian chiefs. The other was Chief Manteo. I remember being on stage during dress rehearsal wearing a headdress, a loincloth and a bunch of body paint that I'd applied myself, my first try at applying body makeup.

Andy smiled down at me and said, "Well, Carl, looks like

North Carolina Collection Photographic Archives

That's Andy, of course, in the upper right. I am in the lower right corner.

you went a little wild with that paint, didn't you?"

"I did?"

"Well, yeah, Carl, maybe just a little bit. I'll show you how to do it later."

After one of our performances, I was thumbing a ride back home to Goldsboro to spend the night with the family. Here came Andy, pulling up in his beat-up old Chevy coupe. It was in such bad shape that when you touched the door handle, you got a shock. If you've ever seen an episode of *The Andy Griffith Show,* you can hear exactly how he sounded when he yelled out the passenger side window with a big toothy smile, "Hey, Carl. Y'all wanna ride?"

I hopped in and he took me home. And he was there again for the ride back. He was just that kind of guy. I was in a Chapel Hill movie theater one evening between shows when I felt a tap on my shoulder. I turned around and there was Andy with his wife, Barbara, who was also in *The Lost Colony*.

"Hey, Carl," he said with that famous grin.

"Hey, Andy," I smiled back.

Andy was also the choir director at a local church — he really had a great singing voice — and to prepare for his *Lost Colony* role each summer, he would start growing a beard in January. As the weeks wore on, he would be looking pretty scroungy, and some of the churchgoers didn't much like it.

Soon after I came home from the army, the woman who ran the boarding house where Andy and I often stayed during *The Lost Colony* passed away. At her funeral, I ran into Barbara. She said, "You will not recognize Andy, Carl. He just finished a movie, *A Face in the Crowd,* directed by Elia Kazan." That role was a surprise to me, but only because I'd lost track of him during my two years of service, not because I didn't think he was good enough to be in a movie of that caliber. If you see that film, you'll realize what a great actor he was.

Barbara and Andy

"Yes," she said, "a movie with Elia Kazan and, Carl, he worked Andy's butt off! His hair is turning gray and he doesn't look the same. But he'll be all right." Andy was more than all right. He went on to do theater, movies and TV, and never forgot his Carolina roots.

I remember talking to Andy

when he was working on a southern version of *Romeo and Juliet*. Of course, Andy's version was a comedy, and when Juliet said, "O Romeo, Romeo! wherefore art thou Romeo?" Romeo popped up and said "I'm right heeeeyeaaarrr!" It was about the same time as Andy's famous "What It Was, Was Football" monologue in November 1953. I was honored to help Andy edit that while I was at the UNC campus station, WUNC. I trimmed it down to a length that would fit on a record. When he performed it live at the Chapel Hill football stadium, I went to see him. I asked, "Is Barbara here?" He pointed and said, "Yes, look over there." I did, and there was Barbara blowing kisses. Of the two of them, we all thought Barbara was the one with the great talent. She could sing, dance, and act, and she was beautiful. The two of them traveled around the region together performing. That led to Andy's big break. At one of their stops, he performed the football monologue, and a talent scout was in the audience. From that, he got the role of Will Stockdale in *No Time for Sergeants*, which ran on Broadway, on TV and as a movie. That's where he and Don Knotts first worked together.

Andy's daughter, Dixie, and I met at a dinner in Chapel Hill a few years ago. We sat and talked about her dad all night long. Of course, Andy was a wonderful actor and musician, but more than being Andy Griffith, the actor, and Andy Griffith, the performer, he was a good friend who would do anything to help me. When I was acting in our high school productions of *Father of the Bride*, *Arsenic and Old Lace* and others, both he and Barbara encouraged me to go into acting, but they understood that my heart was in radio. Dixie told me how proud her father was of me and what I was doing in life and with my career, and that he felt good knowing that he helped just a little in getting me there. Oh, it was more than just a little.

On July 3, 2012, Andy passed away at age 86 from a heart

attack in his home on the Roanoke Sound, not far from where we performed in *The Lost Colony*. When I heard the news, I just sat there and cried. I had lost a dear friend. I just loved the guy.

One of the people responsible for Andy becoming a teacher at Goldsboro High was our drama teacher, Clifton Britton. He was a stage manager and later associate director of *The Lost Colony*, and encouraged Andy to apply for the teaching job. Clifton — "Mr. B."— was a wonderful teacher and helped me understand the importance of projecting my voice. He told us, "The person sitting at the back of the theater paid the same amount of money as the guy in the front row. This person has to hear every word you say, distinctly and beautifully." "Mr. B" had a knack for connecting with us kids. He treated us like adults and expected us to respond as adults. His dedi-

Clifton Britton

Clifton Britton's high school drama group, the Goldmasquers, was, by far, the most popular extracurricular activity at Goldsboro High School. Over 200 students joined the Goldmasquers each year, and I was proud to be elected president of the group my senior year.

LEFT: *"Mr. B." became a great friend. Clara adored him and we were honored that he agreed to be Joe's godfather. This was taken at Joe's baptism at St. Mary's Catholic Church in Goldsboro in 1960.*

cation and professionalism made the school's drama department one of the best in the South. Thousands of drama students, the Goldmasquers, were under his direction in the '40s, '50s and '60s and won numerous competitions against other drama clubs across the state. A talented playwright in his own right, he wrote a play for the community about the Nativity called *A Shepherd's Song*, and the high school performed it each year. It was a beautifully done play, and one year we staged it on the outdoor terrace of a downtown hotel so people on the street below could watch. Over the years, *A Shepherd's Song* has been seen by more than 100,000 people.

"Mr. B" also ran the campus radio department and, as with the theater, paid attention to even the smallest details. That way, if we went on to work in the business, we wouldn't be awed by the professional studios or theaters.

While I loved the opportunities to perform, my desire was always to be on the radio. When I was 16, my voice had matured and I got a part-time job at WGBR, a commercial station in Goldsboro. Before long, I hosted a late evening music show, *Night Dreams,*

43

CARL RAY KASELL
"The world turns aside for the man to pass who knows where he is going."

S.A. Vice-Pres 3; N.C.S.C.C. Vice-Pres 4; National Delegate to NASC 4: S.A. Rep 1; Chm. of Assembly Comm. 3; Class Parlia. 1, 2, 3, 4; Latin Club Vice-Pres 2; Marshal 4; N.H.S. 4; Gmqrs Pres. 4.

My senior photo and list of activities in the 1952 Goldsboro High School yearbook. Perhaps it's worth noting that as Class Parliamentarian for each of my four years, I was laying the foundation for my ascent to be Official Score-keeper and Judge of Wait Wait...Don't Tell Me!

playing romantic songs and waxing poetic about young lovers. In my senior year of high school, I got up early and worked from 6 a.m. until 8:30 a.m. before someone picked me up to take me to school. I'd often find my way back there after school. They had me doing a little bit of everything, but mostly I was a DJ. Doing news wasn't of much interest to me. I wanted to play records and have fun.

My mentor at WGBR was Vassie Balkcum. He was a well-known announcer and radio pioneer in eastern North Carolina and worked his way up from announcer at WGBR to general manag-

Vassie Balkcum

er and majority owner of the station, and of WEQR, the first FM station in eastern North Carolina. Vassie taught me everything I know about how to be on the radio: how to use a microphone, how to read a commercial, and how to simultaneously read a commercial and cue up the next record on the turntable, even if I couldn't hear the needle on the record. Vassie taught me how to feel in my fingertips the slight vibration of the needle when it found the groove where the music started. Then, I would rotate the turntable counterclockwise a few inches so that when I was finished reading the commercial, I could start the turntable and the music would begin immediately. It was a great honor for me in 2004 when Vassie and I were inducted into the North Carolina Halls of Fame. I wasn't the only one of Vassie's announcers to go on to wider fame. Johnny Grant, the longtime ceremonial mayor of Hollywood, began his career as a news announcer at WGBR in 1939.

Grandmother Ida Kasell gave me enough money to get started at the University of North Carolina at Chapel Hill, where the cockiness I had developed as a "radio star" in my small hometown

University Archives, Wilson Library, The University of North Carolina at Chapel Hill

Charlie Kuralt, left, with me at age 18, as WUNC-FM was about to go live for the first time in 1953

didn't last long. There were many very talented broadcasters there, and probably the most gifted was a young man from Charlotte who majored in history and wanted to be a writer. But he had won a national high school speaking contest and did some work on a radio station in Charlotte, and when I heard him on the campus station, I knew immediately that I wasn't nearly as good as I thought I was and had a lot of work to do. His name was Charlie Kuralt and the two of us helped put the campus FM radio station on the air. The AM station had been in operation since the 1940s. On March 13, 1953, Charlie and I stepped up to the microphone in Swain Hall for WUNC's inaugural FM broadcast. We performed a 20-minute drama. Part of my opening script went like this:

From the University of North Carolina, the Communications Center presents a special program written for radio by John Clayton and produced as part of the ceremony dedicating the new university station, WUNC. This is a show about a man who wants to broadcast over the air. About any man. About every man. About all men who have ever dedicated a program, inaugurated a show, gone on the air for the first time ...

Remarkably, the full ceremony and program have been preserved and can be heard on the WUNC website: *www.wunc.edu.*

Charlie and I went on to be part of producing and performing a series called *American Adventure II*, which was the first public radio production to be heard by a national audience. We took real events, like the Valentine's Day Massacre in Chicago, and dramatized them. The NBC Radio Network carried the series coast-to-coast in 1955.

Because it was an educational station, WUNC could only be on the air from 7 p.m. to 11:30 p.m., and could be heard in a whopping 20-mile radius. Working there was a tremendous learning experience because we had the freedom to experiment. We just kept trying things to see what worked, from music to lectures at Memorial Hall. Al Capp and Aldous Huxley were among the speakers we had on.

The station went off the air for six years in 1970 because of some technical difficulties and returned in 1976 as a National Public Radio affiliate and, once again, I was being heard on the WUNC frequency.

Charlie was a master writer who could make you laugh in one sentence and cry in the next. Of course, he went on to have an amazing career at CBS, including as the first anchor of *Sunday Morning*, but his *On the Road* series is what many people remember most. I went along with him once, and we drove into a town where there were signs everywhere saying, "Welcome Home, Joe Smith!" "Glad to have you back, Joe Smith!" I asked Charlie, "I wonder who Joe Smith is?"

He said, "I don't know, let's stop and find out."

Charles Kuralt, 1952

Charlie walked around and talked to everyone he could and listened to stories about Joe Smith. Then he said, "Okay, let's go."

I asked, "Don't you want to meet Joe Smith?"

He said, "No, I think we already know everything we need to know about Joe Smith after talking to the people who know and love him." And he wrote a beautiful story about Joe Smith.

During my college career, I became operations manager for WUNC and, as an announcer, read news and sports scores, including those of UNC basketball games. I'm a huge Tar Heels fan and I briefly considered a career as a sports announcer. I had a short stint as one when Charlie and I were working at a local Chapel Hill commercial station, WCHL, a 1,000-watt station at 1360 AM. It was owned by Sandy McClamroch, who went on to become the town's longest-serving mayor. I went to morning classes and worked afternoons at the station. Charlie did the play-by-play for UNC's baseball games, but had to be gone for a period of time. The program director asked me if I had ever done sports. "Oh, sure, lots of it," I lied, figuring it couldn't be too difficult. So I filled in for Charlie and called a couple of baseball games.

We also voiced a number of commercials, which were often like short radio plays. Below is the 1953 script of "Variety Vacationland."

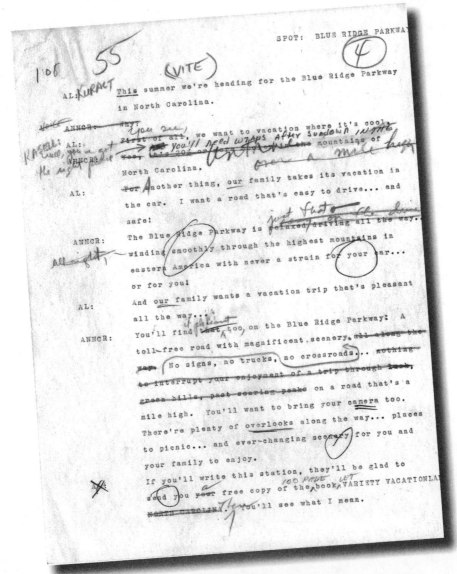

University Archives, Wilson Library, The University of North Carolina at Chapel Hill

Also at WUNC, I had the chance to be part of one of the first "stereo" broadcasts, but oh my, it was crude. We were planning to broadcast a musical performance and worked out a partnership with WCHL to set up a microphone on either side of the performers. One side was broadcast on WUNC and the other on WCHL. We told listeners to turn on two radios, place them on opposite sides of a room, one tuned in to WUNC and the other to WCHL. That was our "stereo." All these years later, when I visit Chapel Hill, someone will come up to me now and then and tell me they heard our first stereophonic effort, and that it worked!

I was fortunate to complete a few years of college before being drafted in 1956. When the army discharged me I went back to Goldsboro, where Vassie Balkcum had a spot waiting for me. I had a morning drive music program, *The Carl Kasell Show.*

"What is it that binds us to this place as to no other? It is not the well or the bell or the stone walls. Or the crisp October nights or the memory of dogwoods blooming. Our loyalty is not only to William Richardson Davie, though we are proud of what he did 200 years ago today. Nor even to Dean Smith, though we are proud of what he did last March. No, our love for this place is based on the fact that it is, as it was meant to be, the University of the people."

— Charles Kuralt at the UNC Bicentennial in 1993

"In the year of '56,
Draft Board got me in this fix!
In the year of '58,
I'll be marching out the gate!"

Part of a drill song chanted by U.S. Army Private
Carl Kasell and his fellow draftees during
Basic Training in 1956

sacramento!

The Korean War ended in 1953, but Uncle Sam was still drafting young men and, in 1956, even though I was still in college, I was one of the chosen. When I reported for my U.S. Army induction exam, they asked if I had skills, and I told them about my radio experience. But at that time, especially if you were drafted, they might have asked what you wanted to do, then told you what you would be doing and where you were going. After my basic training at Fort Jackson, South Carolina, and military school at Fort Gordon, Georgia, the army sent me to the Pentagon for six weeks. Then it was off to northern Italy, where I worked in the communications office for the army's Southern European Task Force for a year and a half. Shortly before I got there, three modern army installations were constructed in the Veneto region of northern Italy

Malcolm Comeaux

The main gate at Caserma Passalacqua in the '50s

on the grounds of old Italian military camps, or "casermas." Each kept the Italian name: mine was Caserma Passalacqua in Verona at the base of the Italian Alps, and, about 40 miles down the road in Vicenza were Caserma Chinotto and Caserma Ederle. Caserma Passalacqua was a fairly large base as I recall, with several thousand U.S. military personnel stationed there.

The Arena di Verona, one of the best preserved of the ancient Roman amphitheaters

Arena di Verona

Verona is a lovely city with the great architecture we associate with ancient European cities. Its origin dates back to a few hundred years B.C., but most of the beautiful buildings still standing when I was there were created in the Middle Ages. One of the largest, and most striking, is the Arena, an amphitheater built in 30 A.D. It is the third largest Roman amphitheater in Italy and has been the stage for great concerts and opera performances. What an amazing experience going there. And the acoustics! They were natural and perfect. There were no microphones or loudspeakers needed, even though the amphitheater seated about 20,000 people. I thought of Andy Griffith and my other actor friends in *The Lost Colony* and in the drama departments at Goldsboro High and UNC, because three of Shakespeare's famous works were set in Verona: *Romeo and Juliet*, *The Two Gentlemen of Verona*, and *The Taming of the Shrew.*

Near the army base was a downtown shopping area. One store sold trinkets and provided money exchange services. A beautiful young employee with black hair and brown eyes caught my eye, and I also noticed that she often walked home alone at night. After several days of admiring her from afar, I stopped by the store and asked if I could walk her home. She said yes, and before long Chiara (Clara in English) De Zorzi and I began going out. I started spending weekends with her and her very large family in their home city of Padua, enjoying their closeness and

Clara and I on a date to the Alps, February 23, 1958

warmth. Over time, we fell in love. When I was scheduled to be sent back to the States, we decided to get married and went to the American consulate for advice on how to go about it. Our contact said, "I have the same situation and I'll tell you exactly what to do. When you go back to the U.S., go to Canada or Mexico, get married and then go to the nearest U.S. embassy or consulate."

The army sent me back to the States and after my discharge, I went home to North Carolina. Vassie Balkcum had a job for me at WGBR, and I resumed my radio career as Clara and I made our long distance plans to be married. It took nearly a year to get everything set. We chose to meet in Mexico rather than Canada, figuring the similarities of Italian and Spanish would make it easier for her. On December 3, 1959, in Mexico City, Clara and I were married. But the long journey wasn't over yet. She had to stay there for about six weeks before all of the paperwork could be completed that would allow her to travel into the United States. In the meantime, I had to

The newlyweds standing in front of the Rectoria Tower of the Universidad Nacional Autónoma de México in Mexico City, December 3, 1959

Joseph Oliver Kasell was born on October 28, 1960.

return to North Carolina to work so I could send her money to live on. When she arrived in Goldsboro, we lived with my family for a while, and they quickly grew to love her, too.

As you can imagine, it couldn't have been easy for Clara to leave her family behind and begin a new life in a small farming community in North Carolina where there were cultural and language barriers. But Clara made friends easily and got a little help from my dad. He asked around at the air base and found an Italian woman living with her husband. Guiliana Lavins became a great friend and eventually became Joe's godmother.

Clara adored her father, Giuseppe, and she made it clear from the first time I met her that if she ever had a son, she would name him after her father. We married on December 3, 1959, and

Joe, at five months, getting a hand from Dad

in October of 1960, here comes a little boy! She had her Giuseppe, or by his American name, Joseph. Clara wanted him to be a doctor or a lawyer, and Joe did get a law degree from George Mason University, but he works as a Systems Engineer at the Naval Federal Credit Union, keeping computers working worldwide. Joe lives in Ashburn, Virginia, with his wife, Lynne, and two daughters, Kathleen Chiara, who was born in 2000 and named for Lynne's mother and Joe's mother, and Katiann, born in 2005.

Clara had difficulty with the English language at times, and when she was frustrated or wanted to make a big statement but couldn't find the words, she'd say, "Sacramento!" Joe and I would respond, "California!" She would say, "Oh, shut up!" And then we would all have a big laugh. She had a great sense of humor, and I see that in Joe, who shares a couple of funny memories about his mother:

One of the ways my mother learned English was by watching TV. She had been watching a commercial for Maxwell House that showed a percolator with music in the background that matched the rhythmic bubbling of the coffee up into the glass top of the pot. So she went to the store to buy the percolator and was expecting it to play music. She was so disappointed when it didn't!

I could tell when my mother was getting upset because she would start saying things in Italian. She was famous for her "Clara Cakes" and one time when she made a special cake for a family member, she took it out of the oven and set it out to cool in the third floor dormer room so my dad and I wouldn't see it. We had a poodle back then, and Mom realized that she hadn't seen him for a while. She started calling for the dog and walked around the house looking for him. As she headed up the stairs, here comes the poodle with face and whiskers covered in cake. Mom peered into the dormer room, saw that half the cake was gone, and started yelling at the dog. It knew it was in trouble and raced downstairs with Mom chasing him, yelling in Italian with some words neither I, nor the dog, had ever heard!

In 1999, Joe and my daughter-in-law, Lynne, traveled with me to Italy. Here, Lynne and I are in Padova, or Padua as it's known in English, Clara's birthplace.

It's hard to describe what you feel when a person you love has cancer. You see all the specialists and with each consultation, a bit of hope slips away until you realize it's a losing battle. When Clara got sick with liver cancer, we went to the best doctors and they did all they could, but there was no beating it. Clara passed away in January of 1997. I was with her the night she died and recall numbly dialing the phone to call a priest. Making that call to Clara's loving family in Italy was so difficult. Losing Clara was a tragedy for our family, and I had never experienced a loss at that level. It came just weeks after my mother passed away. Mother had a difficult time of it at the end, too, suffering a stroke and going blind, and all of us kids pitched in the best we could to help with her care. I was going down to Goldsboro every third or fourth week, leaving DC after work on a Friday and coming back on Sunday. My sister Mary took on the role of primary caretaker for our mother and did a wonderful job helping her through it.

That was a blank time in my life, and I spent a lot of it just sitting on the couch in front of the TV. Had it not been for my job at NPR and the efforts of some of my great friends there, like Jean Cochran and Barry Gordemer, I'm not sure I would have made it out of the house much.

And Joe; oh, how he loved his mother.

Around 1996, my mom started feeling some pain in her torso and had recurring backaches. We thought it might be a disc problem. But they found a tumor growth on her liver. Surgery would be the next step to remove the tumor and we were optimistic; we thought things would be okay. Once the surgeons got in there, they saw that the tumor was larger than they thought, and they really couldn't do anything else for her. She tried chemotherapy, lost weight, lost some of her hair and got weaker and weaker. Mom lasted six months, and her death was just after Grandmother Kasell had passed away. It was a double whammy, an emotional hit for our whole family.

Dad mostly hid how he was feeling, but the morning of

My son, Joe, and my granddaughters, Kathleen, left, and Katiann, 2014

the day Mom died I saw him fall apart. It was the only time, but when you see your father like that, it's a shock, even at 36 years old. It was just so much for him, losing his mother and then his wife.

Clara's death taught me a lot about grief. Everyone grieves differently and experiences it in their own way and on their own timetable. There is no right way to grieve. Well-meaning friends will try to make it easier, but you need to find your own way to the other side. You are left with grief so raw that your heart will seem broken beyond repair, but having that capacity to have loved so deeply is actually what heals you. And, little by little, as what was left behind after 37 years of devotion to one person fades away, you begin to understand that you will come through it. And waiting for you on the other side can be an opportunity to love deeply again. That's how it worked for me, even though there were times I doubted it would. As you'll read a bit later in this book, Mary Ann Foster came into my life thanks to a bit of magic.

I am sure that if Clara were alive today, she would love watching the little granddaughters dancing, especially every November in The Nutcracker. I would love to take the girls to Italy someday and show them Verona and Padova so they can understand where their grandmother came from, and show them the beautiful Italian architecture.

My son, Joe, and I in 2014 at my final Wait Wait *show in Washington, DC*

memories from
joseph kasell

"Could you possibly be related to Carl Kasell?" I get that a lot, and it goes way back. I had an early awareness that Dad was special. I was about the only little kid in Goldsboro with his father's name on a billboard. My friends would tell me when they found out Dad was on the radio, "That has to be cool!" It was, but I realized as the years went by that there is a certain celebrity attached to it by others that I don't experience. For me, having a "rock star" dad has just always been part of my life.

Dad worked hard to take care of his family. There were many years when he worked one radio job in the morning and another in the afternoon. During the years he worked at WAVA, he got up at 4:30 a.m., and then much earlier when he started doing *Morning Edition,* and his sleep patterns were in shifts. But it should come as no surprise to his fans who admired his rock-steady presence on the air that Dad was the same with his off-air family; he was always there for us and always made time for us. He picked me up from school in the afternoons and we played catch in the backyard. He never missed my Little League games. He took me to Washington Senators games. He helped me with homework and took me to Boy Scout meetings. On weekends, we would take rides out to Skyline Drive in the Blue Ridge Mountains, or to Annapolis, or just out to see friends.

Our extended family included loving and active grandparents on both sides. I'm named after my mother's parents. My first name, Joe, is after my grandfather, Giuseppe De Zorzi, and my middle name, Oliver, is for my grandmother, Oliva. Grandpa and Grandma Kasell were big influences in my first five years of life, before we moved from Goldsboro to Virginia. My grandfather would frequently pick me up and take me to Herman Park, located in the middle of Goldsboro. It had a playground and the Kiwanis miniature train driven by a conductor that's still operating today. I loved it, and even after we moved, my grandfather would call and say, "Joe, want to go to the park?" Another thing about him that sticks in my memory is that he never left the house without wearing a hat. He and Grandma Kasell looked tremendous putting on their Sunday best for church.

Food is a major part of my childhood memories. Both of my grandmothers were tremendous cooks. Grandmother Lela Kasell would always make big country breakfasts, and when we spent the night at their house, I woke up to the smells of bacon and grits, and the biscuits were piled high. Grandmother De Zorzi came over from Italy several times to visit and cooked up her pasta specialties, all of which were served in huge portions. My mother made lasagna that would just melt in your mouth, and she followed her mother's example with gigantic helpings. No one in our house, including guests at dinner parties, went hungry.

My mom came from a culturally rich area of Italy and had also lived in Rome, where she worked at the Indonesian Embassy. And here she was, living 4,500 miles away from home in a small farming community in North Carolina, where there were significant cultural differences, not to mention the language barrier. But our family, and the town, were so open and welcoming, and my mother and her mother did well with everyone. Goldsboro was the kind of "Mayberry-ish" place where you could leave your door open at night and people helped each other.

One of the sounds of my early childhood was the Carl Kasell radio jingle. I heard it all the time in my first five years when he was on WGBR. Years later in Washington, around 1979 or 1980, C-SPAN set up cameras at NPR for an inside look at public radio. They started with *Morning Edition* and showed moments leading up to my dad's first newscast of the day. As the video shows him walking into his studio, the engineer started playing his old radio jingle in the background, and my jaw just hit the ground. I hadn't heard it for years.

When Dad did his final newscast for public radio, it was a big celebration, and he invited me to come to the studio and watch. Right before he went into the broadcast booth, I went up to him and said, "Remember, Dad, the word is pronounced 'Chicago.'" This was a tip of the hat to the first episode of *The Mary Tyler Moore Show* when Lou Grant, reviewing the previous broadcast, was stunned that Ted Baxter had mispronounced "Chicago." *Mary Tyler Moore* and *WKRP in Cincinnati* were two of his favorite shows, and we enjoyed watching them together. The characters on both of the programs are somewhat embellished composites, but we've seen each one of the characters at one or more of the stations he worked at, especially Herb, the salesman on *WKRP.* We got a good laugh out of those programs.

People ask me about my dad retiring at 80. We all should be so lucky to find something we love doing and be able to do it for so long. Dad grew up with radio; it was in his blood and he's so comfortable behind a microphone. And he was so good at it.

To this day, people ask if I'm related to Carl Kasell. I couldn't be prouder to answer, "Yes, I am. He's my father."

If you work at something for a long time, you might wind up in a museum. That's what happened to me at the Wayne County Museum, in Goldsboro, North Carolina. There are many great exhibits there. You should stop in sometime.

— milestones —

"On Friday, the United States Supreme Court will welcome its first female justice. That became assured yesterday with the Senate confirmation of Sandra O'Connor. NPR's Nina Totenberg has the story."

October 6, 1981

"Good morning, I'm Carl Kasell. Egypt's president Sadat was shot at today while watching a military parade in Cairo. Jim Lederman has been monitoring the situation from Jerusalem."

— four—

now pitching, carl kasell!

My love of baseball, and of the St. Louis Cardinals, goes back to the 1946 World Series when the Cardinals defeated the Boston Red Sox in seven games. I listened to the play-by-play on the radio as a North Carolina boy, Enos "Country" Slaughter, made a great dash from first base on a single to score the winning run for the Cardinals. I've always liked their uniform, too, with the bat across the chest.

Joe shares my love of baseball, and we were both broken-hearted when the Washington Senators and our heroes like Frank Howard departed for Texas after the 1971 season. Team owner Bob Short became the most hated man in Washington, and that's quite an accomplishment in this town. No one believed that we would ever really lose the Senators. I mean, who could possibly imagine the nation's capital without the national pastime?

Bob Short could.

And then we had to suffer through a string of broken promises that another team would soon be here. Year after year we kept hoping that we would get a team, and rumor after cruel rumor only poured salt on our wound. Bowie Kuhn didn't help matters. The Commissioner of Baseball (until 1984) promised that Major League

Baseball would be back at RFK Stadium by 1978. It wasn't.

Our hopes were raised high again in 1991 when baseball decided to add two teams to the National League. The commissioner sent an expansion committee to town to inspect old RFK and judge whether we were franchise-worthy. Miami, Tampa, Buffalo and Denver were the other cities being considered. Nothing against those other fine cities and their wonderful NPR listeners, but how could Washington not be chosen? Astoundingly, it wasn't; Miami and Denver were. Defeated, we realized it would take a minor miracle to get a team back in Washington.

But the miracle came. Finally, our 34-year nightmare ended in 2005 when the struggling Montreal Expos franchise was moved to Washington. The team would not be the Senators, though; the mayor of DC objected to that name because the District of Columbia does not have representation in the Senate. So, the Washington Nationals took the field and baseball was back at RFK Stadium. A few years later, the Nationals moved to their sparkling new stadium. Joe and his family live about 45 minutes away from us and he'll often call and say, "Dad, let's go to a ballgame." And we do. There's nothing like sitting at a ballgame with my son. Grab a cold drink, maybe some popcorn, and sit back and watch the game. After the Senators abandoned us, I still had the Cardinals to cheer for.

In 2010, *Wait Wait* was doing a show in St. Louis and I was asked to throw out the ceremonial first pitch at one of their games. First pitch in Busch Stadium! I called Joe to tell him, and his response was, "You've got to be kidding me!" And, it was funny, because he started coaching me, going over the things I had taught him years ago, like putting your fingers across the seam. And, "Dad, don't you dare bounce the ball! And don't stand on the mound; you need to stand on the edge of the grass in front of the mound and throw it high."

"Okay, son. I'll do it." I was able to practice a little with one of the players under the stands beforehand which made it easier when I got out to the field. My catcher was David Freese, who went on to become the World Series MVP in 2011, and I got to meet Cards manager Tony LaRussa in the dugout. After the announcer introduced me at home plate, I walked toward the mound and followed Joe's instructions. I reared back and threw that ball right over the plate for a strike!

It was one of those nearly indescribable moments of a lifetime, such a thrill. When you're a longtime baseball fan and you get a chance to do that, well, wow! And it happened to me again when I was asked to throw out a first pitch in Cincinnati when the Reds played the Yankees. Again, I followed Joe's advice and put one

Cincinnati Reds

Being greeted by Rosie Redlegs after throwing out the first pitch in Cincinnati

across the plate. I felt good about my throw, and as I started to walk back to the dugout, Rosie Redlegs came running up to me and threw her arms around my neck. I thought it was to congratulate me for my great pitch. Instead, I heard a young woman's voice from inside the big mascot head say, "Carl Kasell, I love your show!" I thanked her and was happy that she was a fan of *Wait Wait*, but couldn't she have said something about the strike I had just thrown?

To give you an idea of how passionate Joe is about baseball, when the Major League players went on strike in 1981, he wrote a letter to the editor that was printed in *Sports Illustrated*. Joe was a junior at George Mason then.

> *As a long-time Washington, DC area resident, I can sympathize with the baseball fans in other parts of the country who are now suffering through an empty summer. I can also understand their bitterness toward players and management. Many of us in this area felt the same way 10 years ago when our beloved Senators were taken away despite our unwavering loyalty. Nobody cared about the fans then and nobody cares now.*
>
> *— Joe Kasell, Alexandria, VA*

That letter made me a very proud father, but then, I've never *not* been proud of Joe.

As a dad, it's a nice feeling when your efforts to provide memorable moments for your young son continue to be acknowledged over the years, even decades later. The following memory from Joe goes back to the late '60s.

> *Through the radio station, WPIK, Dad was able to get us*

press passes now and then to see the Senators play at RFK Stadium. I was able to meet some of the players, which, for a little kid, was a huge thrill. I was playing Little League then, and Dad was almost always home from work in the afternoons and could help me with throwing and hitting, and he always came to my games. We had this bond with baseball. After we went to the last ever Senators game, we were a little lost without a hometown team. Sometimes we'd make trips to Baltimore and Philadelphia to watch National League games, but it wasn't the same. We picked up where we left off with the Nationals and I've had partial season tickets from the first year.

Some of my earliest sports memories involve sitting in front of the TV with Dad in the late '60s watching University of North Carolina basketball games. One of the stories he told me was about watching the 1957 national championship game on TV with Pat Howell, a radio pal of his. The

Ten-year-old Joe with starting pitcher Dick Bosman at RFK in 1971, the Senators final season

semi-final against Michigan State went to triple overtime before the Tar Heels won 74-70. The final was against Kansas and featured a sophomore phenom named Wilt Chamberlain. The game was in Kansas City and was practically a home game for the Jayhawks, who were favored despite UNC's higher ranking in the polls and unbeaten season. But the Tar Heels won, again in triple overtime, 54-53. Dad often talked about that game and the team led by Coach Frank McGuire and star players like Lennie Rosenbluth. Coach McGuire left in 1961 to coach the Philadelphia Warriors and was replaced with the Carolina coach who brought us many great teams over the next 36 years, Dean Smith. The photo below with Coach Smith is one my father and I will forever cherish.

LEFT TO RIGHT: *Legendary UNC coach Dean Smith with me and my son Joe*

In the late 1980s, UNC was in the NCAA tournament and there was a second round game against Michigan. As was common in those days, because of the number of tourna-

ment games being played simultaneously, television cover-age was regionally-based, meaning that the UNC/Michigan game was not being broadcast in the DC area. That week-end, however, my dad was visiting with my grandmother in Goldsboro, which meant he could watch the game on the sta-tion located in Raleigh. So what did he do? He watched the game while providing me the play-by-play over the phone. You do what you have to do.

In 1982, Dad bought tickets to the Final Four in New Orleans. UNC was picked by many as the preseason favor-ite to win it all, and they didn't disappoint us. It was a tre-mendous trip as we had the chance to visit New Orleans for several days, and to witness the first Final Four to be played in the Superdome. Our seats were in the last row of the up-per deck, but we really didn't care. All we remember was the winning shot being made by a skinny freshman named Mi-chael Jordan against a strong Georgetown team. Even with that shot, there was still time left for Georgetown, until they threw the ball away to future NBA great James Worthy. As the last seconds were winding down, my dad was jumping up for joy while I was still "coaching" and yelling at Worthy to run out the clock. That was a great moment.

Among the many perks of working at NPR was the occa-sional visit to the studios of a baseball legend who was promoting his recently published book. Generally, I would have a day's notice, which usually meant an urgent phone call to Joe asking, "Where's the baseball?" The baseball was the one, which later became sev-eral, that had autographs of many Baseball Hall-of-Famers. Among the legends who I met and whose autographs I still have are Hank

Aaron, Willie Mays, Stan Musial, Duke Snyder, Yogi Berra, Warren Spahn, and Bob Feller.

Melody Kramer

Moose Skowron, an All-Star for many years mostly with the Yankees and White Sox, was a guest on Wait Wait *in 2008. He let me try on his 1961 Yankees World Series ring.*

Another Baseball Hall-of-Famer who was a regular on *Morning Edition* was Red Barber. Bob Edwards' weekly four-minute conversations with the sportscasting legend were a treasure and something to look forward to each week. Red did the play-by-play from the 1930s through the 1960s for the Reds, Brooklyn Dodgers, and Yankees. For a dozen years he and Bob — called the "Kentucky Colonel" by Red because of Bob's native state — would talk each week about sports. Just as often, they would talk about literature, or music, or theater, or how the camellias were doing outside Red's home in Tallahassee, Florida.

In the early years of *Morning Edition*, I filled in for Bob when he was away, and one of those times happened to fall on a Red Barber Friday. It was June of 1983, and each of our NPR commentators had been asked to prepare their remarks as if they were giving advice to college graduates. Red, in his always quiet, thoughtful way, said college graduates weren't the ones we should be talking to. He said we should be telling children as they are starting school that the most important thing they can do, their job, is to get an education. He said it should be a broad education including the liberal arts, but most importantly, reading. Red said if you get out into the world and you can't read, "you are in the pickle vat." No one could tell a story like Red Barber.

Red died in 1992 at the age of 84. A year later, Bob published a wonderful tribute, *Fridays with Red: A Radio Friendship*, based on those *Morning Edition* conversations.

What does it take to be good on the air? You have to remember what you're there to do. You are passing on information about the world, not trying to be a star. Focus on the message and your personality will come along naturally.

Write it well, and read it so it is understandable. Imagine that you're just sitting in a room with someone, a friend, telling them a story in plain language. Be yourself. It's very simple, very effective.

elvis and katie couric

Many radio stations in the '50s and '60s used elaborately orchestrated jingles to introduce and promote their disc jockeys. Big bands and singers were used; they were quite the productions. Here were the lyrics to the jingle that WGBR produced for my show:

> It's "The Carl Kasell Show," with tops in tunes in Golds-
> boro radio. Carl Kasell plays the best tunes that are your
> favorite requests; 1-1-5-0, Carl Kasell's show.
> "The Carl Kasell Show."

Radio has changed a lot since then. Devoting that much time and expense to a disc jockey's introduction is mostly unheard of now. The '50s was also a different era for record promotion. Many singers who were touring in our area would just drop by the radio station to try to get us to play their records. One young man, just as polite as you could imagine, handed me his record and said, "Sir, I'd appreciate it if you'd play my record a few times. Maybe the audience would hear it and maybe someone might buy it. I'd sure appreciate it if you'd do that. And I thank you very much, sir."

"You say your name is what?" I asked.

"Presley, sir. Elvis Presley."

We found out later that when he wasn't promoting his reccords at little radio stations like ours, he liked to go to the local movie theaters and sing a few of his songs between films. Soon he started selling out his concerts, and I remember thinking, he's got a great voice, but what the heck does he have now that he didn't have before? I believe that would have been in the spring of 1955, because it was before Elvis appeared on TV in 1956 with the Dorsey Brothers on CBS' *Stage Show* and started twisting and shaking those hips, making the girls go crazy. The rest is history.

In 1960, when Clara joined me in Goldsboro and little Joe came along, I continued my morning show at WGBR but knew that I would eventually need to make a better salary to support my growing family, and that meant going to a larger market. We were doing okay in Goldsboro, but Clara suggested that my career opportunities would be greater in a bigger city. She enjoyed Goldsboro but came from a fairly big city in Italy, lived and worked in Rome for a while, and always dreamed of living in a large city rich in culture again. She got her wish when we moved to the Washington area.

In 1965, I took a job as a morning drive disc jockey at WPIK in Alexandria, Virginia, playing a little bit of everything: country and western, pops, jazz. In the mid-morning we played what was called "music for the housewives." But I was still looking for additional income when a friend working at WAVA in Arlington, one of the first "all-news" stations in the country, called me and said they had a part-time opening on the weekends reading news. That friend was Jim Russell, who shares some of his memories:

In 1965, almost 50 years ago, I was a kid who had dropped out of college to try out radio as a career. I lived in Washington, DC, and I contacted every single radio station in that area, but nobody would hire someone who had no

*real experience. So finally, I did what I needed to — I lied
and said I did have experience. An AM music station in Alexandria, Virginia, WPIK, hired me and told me to report for
work two weeks later. When I arrived, the station manager
pulled me into his office.*

*"We checked your references and they weren't real. So,
we've hired a real professional instead."*

And he introduced me to Carl Kasell.

*When I asked the station manager if he had anything I
could do, he said, "Sure, you can do the news." And, although my voice was terrible to start with, so bad that some
of the DJs begged me to let them read their own news, Carl
took pity on me and taught me radio. He was a very generous
guy in that way, and took me under his wing.*

*About a year and a half later, I went to work at another
station, WAVA in Arlington, the self-proclaimed first all-
news station in the country. I recruited Carl to come with me.
He did and went on to become the station's news director.*

Jim went on to become a legend in public radio programming and, for many years, has been a creative consultant with his
own company, which you can read more about at www.theprogram-
doctor.com. Among many other career highlights, he created the
public radio business show *Marketplace*, which reaches nearly 10
million listeners across the United States.

But back to 1966. While I was grateful to Jim for the WAVA
offer, I wasn't that interested because I didn't really want to do news.
I wanted to be an entertainer. That's why radio appealed to me in the
first place. But I was getting the feeling that the music was getting
past me. Rock was developing an edge that I didn't care for. And I

needed the money. I was able to keep the WPIK job during the week and anchored the news on WAVA on weekends.

Just as rock music was changing, the turbulence of the late sixties brought a string of big news stories. Being able to report on them from the nation's capital and being close to so many of the events and newsmakers was fascinating.

In June of 1967, the Middle East exploded with the Six-Day War between Israel and its Arab neighbors, where Israeli troops took control of the Gaza Strip. As I write this 47 years later, Gaza violence is still in the headlines. There were Vietnam War demonstrations every weekend with the first big one, over 100,000 strong, in October of that year. In April of 1968, Martin Luther King, Jr. was assassinated, which was followed by riots and fires in Washington. Our studios were on a high enough floor that I could look out and see the smoke and flames, a sobering sight. Two months later, Bobby Kennedy was murdered. In 1972, Watergate came along, and then the resignation of President Nixon.

There were many other big stories over the years and it was a great learning period for me, because when I was in college, I majored in English and never bothered with classes in the radio-TV department. I thought my two years of work at WGBR during high school taught me all I needed to know. That on-the-job training at WAVA when so much was happening was an education that no amount of tuition could have bought. So, firmly hooked on news, I had forgotten all about playing records and left the housewives behind. I felt that news was going to be it, and I became a full-time newsman at WAVA.

Eventually, I was promoted to news director at WAVA and, in 1976, I received a note from the station owner. He wrote, "I have a friend of the family who has a daughter going to school at the

CARL KASELL
News Director

This is how I looked in the early '70s at WAVA.

University of Virginia, studying journalism. She wants to be a broadcaster. She would like to come here and be an intern this summer. If you'd like some free help, she's available." And he emphasized "free." So I dialed the number on the note and the young woman answered. We chatted briefly, and I asked her to come by the station for an interview.

She did, and after chatting for a while I found her to be really sharp and eager to learn. So I asked Katie Couric if she wanted to be my intern. She worked with us that summer, then went back to college in the fall. She returned in November to help us out during the elections. Great gal! She brought life to that newsroom.

In 1998, Willard Scott came by NPR to record something for us. We sat and talked for a while and I asked him how Katie was doing. She had recently lost her husband, Jay Monahan, to colon cancer at the age of 42.

"Oh, I think she's doing pretty well," said Willard. "I'll see her tomorrow morning."

"Well, tell her I said hello."

"I'll do it!" he said.

On *The Today Show* the next morning, Willard finished his weather forecast and said, "Katie, I was in Washington yesterday at NPR and ran into an old friend of ours, Carl Kasell. He said to tell you hello."

Within a few minutes, my phone was ringing. One of my sisters called, all excited, out of breath, and said, "Carl, did you see TV this morning? Did you see Willard and Katie talking about you?"

Several other people called and e-mailed me about it asking, "Did you see? Did you see?" I never did see the video. It was kind of amusing how thrilled so many people were about my name being mentioned on *The Today Show* when you consider that many millions more people heard my voice every morning on *Morning Edition.*

In early June of 2014, Mary Ann and I flew to New York. Katie invited me on her ABC Television talk show, where we chatted about old times. On a personal note, I was so happy that Katie found love again and was married just a couple of weeks after I was on her show. She's a sweetheart.

KatieCouric.com

— milestones —

"Good morning, I'm Carl Kasell. Memorial services are being held today in Concord, New Hampshire, the hometown of Christa McAuliffe. She was among the seven crewmembers aboard the space shuttle Challenger who were killed yesterday when the space ship exploded just after liftoff from Cape Canaveral."

November 9, 1989

"From National Public Radio news in Washington, I'm Carl Kasell. West German Chancellor Helmet Kohl flew home today, interrupting a visit to Poland. The chancellor made his decision following yesterday's development in East Germany in which the Berlin Wall was opened. His first stop is West Berlin."

The most important part of reporting a breaking news story to your listeners is getting it right, not being first. Countless mistakes have been made by broadcasters trying to "scoop" the competition. One example that affected me personally happened on March 4, 2014, when NPR announced that I would be leaving my job as official judge and scorekeeper of *Wait Wait*. A radio industry magazine picked up the story and sent an e-mail to its subscribers in which it reported that I had passed away.

Not so fast ...

Barry Gordemer

Here I am, caught sneaking a peek at Mary Ann Foster minutes after we first met. She and I were assigned to the same table at Barry Gordemer's wedding reception at the London Zoo in August of 1998. The man in the middle is famed British magician Paul Daniels, the emcee.

— six —

meeting mary ann

After Clara died in 1997, I didn't give much thought to meeting someone new. I was in my 60s and assumed I would spend the rest of my life alone. I didn't, as you know, but how I got from thinking I would, to entertaining the idea that I might find love again was an interesting process. In many ways, my son Joe and I had put our lives on hold during Clara's ordeal, and I'll let him tell things from his perspective.

Dad's advice to me the evening after my mom passed was to move forward with my life. He said that we weren't thinking of anything but her health for so long, but now she was gone and he told me to move on. And I did. A couple of months later, I proposed to Lynne and she said yes. And the wedding and the expectation of grandchildren became something new for Dad and me to look forward to. Of course, we grieved and the void was there, and we thought of many things my mom was missing out on.

While I was moving on, I was concerned that Dad wasn't. I realized he was a big boy and he'd eventually be fine, but I needed to make sure he was okay. He was so lucky to have radio during that time to at least get him out of the house, and one of his radio friends, Barry Gordemer, not only got him out of the house, he got him out of the country.

Barry Gordemer and I shared a love of magic, which I write about in Chapter Nine. In addition, Barry loved puppetry and built puppets for ventriloquists, for video projects and for customers all over the world, including NPR. In 1999, it commissioned a Bob Edwards puppet to commemorate *Morning Edition*'s 20th anniversary. He's very talented and that went over well, so NPR asked him to make one for me, which is shown in the *Wait Wait* chapter, and for several other NPR people.

Three of Barry Gordemer's NPR puppets; He also made ones of Robert Siegel, Noah Adams, the Car Talk guys, Peter Sagal and others.

As Barry will explain, his puppet business led to Mary Ann and I meeting.

Mary Ann Foster's son, Brian, was a puppeteer in the Washington area and was one of my customers. Over the years, we became very good friends. When Amy and I decided to get married in 1998, we wanted to have our wedding in London. I had family there, and being in the magic business, Amy had traveled to London often and had many friends there. We invited Brian and his mother, and among my NPR friends, we invited Carl.

One of the toughest parts about getting married is the

seating chart. The marriage is easy compared to the trauma of the seating chart. You want to put people together who will be comfortable. I've been at wedding receptions and sat in awkward silence where after everyone at the table introduced themselves, no one would know what to say next. So we decided that every table at our wedding would have a good conversation starter, and the way the math worked out, one table would have two conversation starters in Carl Kasell and Mary Ann Foster.

Mary Ann is a therapist and a natural in communicating with people and, of course, Carl is Carl. They're both very good conversationalists; they're people that the moment you meet them, you feel like you've known them for 30 years. So we thought it would be perfect to seat them at the same table. We had no idea what we were about to get started.

The next day, we did a cruise down the Thames and Carl and Mary Ann sat next to each other, and they hit it off, I guess. They started dating almost immediately after that.

You're welcome, Carl.

As they say, timing is everything, and from the perspective of my being ready to get off the couch and do something other than just going to work, it was nearly perfect timing when I went to Barry and Amy's wedding. I was immediately interested in Mary Ann. She was strikingly beautiful with a great personality. We seemed to hit it off despite our great differences. She had been single for over 30 years and I had been happily married for nearly 40 years. She had held a variety of positions, including director of marketing for a financial institution, before going back to get her master's degree in social work and entering private practice; I had one career.

Mary Ann had traveled the world, her wanderlust probably fueled at an early age by the free rail travel her family received because her father worked for the Southern Railroad. I worked a lot and stayed pretty close to home. Oh, I had been to Italy a few times, thanks to Uncle Sam at first, and then trips to see Clara's family later. But Mary Ann was a globetrotter compared to me.

We did have a couple of things in common: We each had one child, a son. She shared at least my interest in, if not my love of, the South. Mary Ann's grandparents lived in Arkansas and she appreciated that wonderful way southern people are so cordial and polite.

Several weeks after the wedding, I was pleased to receive an invitation from Mary Ann to have dinner at her place along with other locals from the wedding party. It wasn't a "date," but it was the closest thing to one that I'd had in about 40 years. I wore a suit and since it was near Halloween, I bought a little porcelain pumpkin and a potted plant for the hostess.

In the early going, I saw Mary Ann only as a potential friend, maybe somebody that I could go to the movies with from time to time. I didn't know how to go about it and wasn't sure about getting into another romantic relationship. I was hesitant because I didn't want to experience a loss like Clara's again. It seemed that Mary Ann had her reservations, too, and we were just hit-and-miss for a while. But before long, we were seeing each other every weekend. Slowly, I realized it was okay; a little giddiness had found its way back into my life and it felt wonderful to realize that life could still be beautiful, even at my advanced age.

This is where I should stop. I recall a news story several years ago about how researchers had proven that while men might be better at remembering tactical details, such as directions or useless trivia, women are far superior when it comes to more emotional

91

memories, like dating and weddings. So here's Mary Ann.

Carl says he was going to call me for dinner, but I don't think he would have. He hadn't dated for 50 years. I was divorced and my ex-husband had died at a young age. My son, Brian, worried about me being alone, and once, at the age of eight, tried to set me up with his doctor. In 1998, he mentioned that through his NPR friend Barry, he had met Carl Kasell, and that he was a really nice guy and that I should get to know him. I didn't really know who Carl was. While I did listen to NPR, I wasn't an avid listener and was more often tuned in to '50s and '60s rock and roll, blues, etc. I loved Elvis, the Beatles and Broadway music. After Brian mentioned Carl, I listened to him on NPR and thought he sounded like a nice person. I didn't think any more about it.

Brian and I planned a month-long trip to Istanbul with a stopover in London to attend Barry and Amy's wedding. And that is where I met Carl. Barry took me over to introduce me to Carl, but Carl was busy taking pictures, so it was a quick hello and that was it. I'm not sure Carl even remembers this. The wedding was wonderful, and the next day everyone went on a cruise down the Thames. I didn't know many people at NPR, so I was sitting by myself. And that's when I really met Carl because he sat next to me and we started talking. We had the best time talking about old movies and the South. We talked a mile a minute. Carl is such a gentleman, a straight arrow. He's so proper and never uses salty language. Maybe he'll utter a "Heck fire!" when he's perturbed, but that's as close as he gets. I'm a little more salty.

More people joined us at our table and we all had a great

time. After the cruise, Brian and others wanted to go to a pub. Carl and I were game, so we joined them and got to know each other better. Brian and I had to catch a plane to Istanbul the next day, so Carl and I hugged goodbye and that was the end of that.

When we returned from Istanbul, I decided to have the Washington people from the wedding over for a dinner party. Carl was part of the group. I still maintain that, at the time, I was only looking for someone to go to the movies with. But perhaps I had something in the back of my mind because I worked days on that dinner to seduce Carl — and it was the last nice dinner I ever made him!

Soon after, I went to a Halloween party at Barry's where Carl and Barry were doing their magician act, and it was so funny. I was wearing a Venetian mask, cape, tights and high black heels for a party I was going to later in the evening. Carl and I went out on the balcony, and he asked if I wanted to go to a movie and get some pizza sometime. We did that, and he then asked me if I would go to see Annie Get Your Gun at the Kennedy Center. A month away! The men I had known in the past would not have asked me out a month in advance. Carl is the last of the southern gentlemen.

Carl said, "You look so startled."

"Well, I am startled, but I'd love to go." That impressed me. He makes and keeps plans and he's on time, which was amazing to me as I was occasionally attracted to the bad boys.

We started doing things regularly on the weekends. Carl lived in Virginia, which was a long drive to my house in Chevy Chase. So he decided he was going to sell his house

When we were dating, Mary Ann and I bought a vacation home together in Warm Springs. Here's one of our neighbors.

and move closer to Washington. He was determined that we were going to see each other and it was going to work. His new place in Glover Park needed updating, and I oversaw the project. During the construction, I told him he could stay with me, but only while his house was being re-done. I liked my solitude and living my life as it was. But it turned out I also loved having Carl there. It was perfect. He moved in and pretty much never left.

When his house was finished, we would spend weekends there and live in my house during the week. I could see that living with someone wasn't as bad as I thought. He was so obliging to do things I like to do, just perfect in a lot of ways. Still, while Carl was the marrying kind, I didn't want to ruin the relationship by getting married.

After we had been dating, someone at NPR referred to him as "the New Carl" because he had changed so much. He became very talkative; his wardrobe changed. Carl told me as we got to know each other that at the time of the wedding, he was just beginning to think that he was going to do some things to change his life. He was ready. Carl was ready to have an adventure.

As Mary Ann mentioned, I'm a bit of a southern gentleman and I needed to ask her son, Brian, for his approval. Here's how he remembers the moment.

One afternoon, Carl took me aside. As we both stood in front of the fireplace, he turned serious.

"Brian, you know your mother and I have been going out for quite a while now."

"Yes, I know."

"I love your mother very much."

"Yes." That was clear to me and to anyone who had been around them.

"Brian, I'd like to ask if you would be okay with me asking for her hand in marriage."

It was a surreal moment. I felt like I was living through an episode of an old black-and-white TV show where the authoritative father figure had pulled me aside for a heart-to-heart talk. It wasn't that I was surprised that Carl wanted to marry my mom, I was just shocked that he was asking for my permission. But here I was, finally getting my mom hooked up with a really sincere, good looking, charismatic guy; plus I would get a surrogate dad out of the deal. What more could I ask for? I gave my "blessing." It made me feel silly as hell, but such is romance, right?!

Mary Ann and NPR's "Roving Ambassador" at one of my speaking engagements

Mary Ann and I started making plans for our 2003 wedding. As for the details, again, I'll graciously bow to the lady of the house.

My dream was to have a simple wedding at home. I have a big backyard and I'm proud of my flower garden with its lovely fountain. We picked May 24th because the spring tulips and azaleas would be out and the rainy season would

THIS JUST IN...

■ Our congratulations to NPR's "Morning Edition" newscaster **Carl Kasell**, who's also "official judge and scorekeeper" for the antic game show "Wait Wait . . . Don't Tell Me," among other duties. The 69-year-old Kasell is getting married May 24 to 62-year-old psychotherapist **Mary Ann Foster**. "Wait Wait" host **Peter Sagal**, the brother of a rabbi, will officiate at the nontraditional ceremony at Oak Hill Chapel in Georgetown, with witnesses expected to include **Bob Edwards** and **Cokie Roberts**. The bride-to-be told us: "Carl is very romantic. He is just so fetching!" Kasell said: "I try to be romantic. . . . She made the first move, of course, inviting me over for dinner. Then later I asked her out." The two, both widowed, met at a wedding in London five years ago when Foster's son, **Brian**, played yenta, urging his mom to chat up the veteran broadcaster.

Our engagement made the Washington Post *on April 23, 2003.*

certainly have passed. I was wrong. It started raining 30 days before and never stopped, except for a little window at 5 p.m. on our wedding day. Definitely a miracle. The sun came out, kind of, and it did stop raining, finally.

We married in the historic Renwick Chapel at the Oak Hill Cemetery in Georgetown. My mom and dad were buried on the grounds, and I had the nice feeling that they were with us in spirit. I am sure Carl felt his parents' presence as well. Both sets of parents would have approved of this marriage. When I walked down the aisle and saw Carl looking so handsome and debonair, I was overwhelmed with the sense of all being right in my world. This was going to be a great day!

It was a warm and relaxed atmosphere with of all of us being literally close together in the tiny chapel. Brian sang Con te Partiro, *the romantic Italian song that made Andrea Bocelli famous. Brian practiced for weeks to get the correct pronunciation and range. He was fantastic! There was not a dry eye in the house. Of course, with Peter Sagal officiating, we had laughter as well, and the marvelous people who helped us were in the mood for a celebration.*

Joe Kasell, Carl's son, was best man. Bob Edwards, Jean Cochran and Adam Felber participated. Patricia Kennedy played the flute, Sonya Hayes the violin, Victoria Gau the viola, and David Rubin the cello. The music was beautiful, especially with the sun finally shining through the stained glass windows, and, again, no rain. Rose and Grace Sagal and Kathleen Kasell were the glamorous flower girls My very best friend, Sandy Brudin, whom I met when I was three in Glover Park, was the matron of honor. She and her sister,

Pat Holman, came to my house early and pasted me together in my pink wedding dress and shoes. We have known each other forever and we spent much of the time laughing at me and my nerves. I felt like a new bride; this was really the first formal wedding for both Carl and me. Each of us was married by a justice of the peace the first time.

After the vows, we sashayed over to my house for a big dinner. My fantasy of being at home and having lovely tables all set up outside in the garden in a very elegant fashion with good food and drink for everyone was fulfilled. Our two white Labradors, Gilda and Sophie, were running around saying hi to the crowd. A band played '40s and '50s songs, like It Had To Be You, *and* Hello Love, La Mer *and* What A Wonderful World, *the tune Louis Armstong did so well and the one Carl and I love most. We also had some Beatles and Elvis tunes when we decided to really get down.*

Carl and I had been taking tango lessons, and we cut quite an impressive rug with our Latin moves. We did a few dips and, amazingly, Carl did not drop me!

Toasts were made, and I gave Carl two kayaks so we could float away down the Cow Pasture River near our vacation home in the mountains of Warm Springs, Virginia. It was a fine reception and, although it did not rain, everyone ruined their shoes dancing around in the mud from the previous month of rain. But our guests were the kind of people who were just happy to be a part of the fun, even with the mud. I was extremely happy.

Brian gave a speech saying he had always been looking for a knight in shining armor to come and be his mother's protector — and went on to say he was sick of mowing my lawn and going places with me! Well, I have a new travel partner, and so does Brian. He married a Hungarian woman, Csilla, and they and their two little children, Rocco and Lydia, lived in Paris until just recently moving back to the U.S.

On our honeymoon, Carl and I went to France, and then we trekked from village to village in the Cinque Terre, a rugged portion along the coast of the Italian Riviera.

One day when we were walking these very high cliffs that overlook the Mediterranean, there was a German group in front of us. It was a one-person path precariously winding along the edge of a steep, rocky drop thousands of feet down the mountain. As we passed them, I stepped around on the uphill side. Carl went around on the downhill side. There were bushes, but when he stepped on one of them, it was just air underneath.

My husband was about to fall off the cliff on our honeymoon! But just in the nick of time, these lovely Germans grabbed him and hauled him up off the cliff. They saved his life. It could have been the end of Carl Kasell. And the end of me; you just don't kill Carl Kasell and come back to the United States and face his adoring fans!

Marriage to Carl has been wonderful. At first, I considered NPR as my major rival because that's all he talked about. But I've gotten to know the people there, and it couldn't be a nicer company and group of people. They've been so kind to Carl over the years and so kind to me. I am very proud of Carl, and I enjoy going on his NPR "Roving Ambassador" trips to Chicago and places beyond with the Wait Wait crew. What a fabulous time we all had together.

People love Carl and they spread that love to me.

My marriage to Mary Ann was a beautiful moment in my life, surrounded by family and friends as we began our new adventure together. I love Mary Ann and I'm so lucky to have met and married her. We have so much fun traveling, going to the movies and theater, and we love to walk our dogs through Rock Creek Park.

NAMES & FACES

Kasell, Foster Tie Knot

Saturday's 5 p.m. nuptials for National Public Radio's veteran news broadcaster began like this: "I'm **Peter Sagal**, with this hour's news. **Carl Kasell** and **Mary Ann Foster** are no longer living in sin."

NPR's star newsman and his psychotherapist fiancee tied the knot at Oak Hill Chapel in Georgetown in front of 100 guests including a number of Kasell's NPR family. **Cokie Roberts, Bob Edwards, Jean Cochran, Liane Hansen, Neal Conan** and the cast and crew of "Wait Wait . . . Don't Tell Me!" were all in attendance, reports The Post's **Roxanne Roberts**. Kasell serves as "Wait Wait's" official judge and scorekeeper; host Sagal presided over the ceremony.

The couple met five years ago at a wedding in London when Foster's son **Brian** recognized Kasell's distinctive baritone. After Brian urged his mother to introduce herself, the couple clicked. This is the second marriage for both, but the first formal wedding for either. The wedding party included their grown children and grandchild.

After a honeymoon in France and Italy, they'll be back to use Foster's wedding present to her groom: his-and-hers kayaks. Updates on the half-hour.

BY BRIAN FOSTER

After Mary Ann Foster and NPR's Carl Kasell were wedded at Oak Hill Chapel in Georgetown, it was off to France and Italy for a honeymoon.

Our wedding announcement in the Washington Post *on May 26, 2003*

100

It's good for the dogs and it's good for us. I couldn't ask for anyone better. Mary Ann is one wonderful woman!

It's funny how things often work out in ways that you least expect. Love found me again when I wasn't looking. Mary Ann and I now have this big, beautiful family with two sons, two daughters-in-law and four grandchildren. I know how pleased Joe was when I started dating Mary Ann. He saw me at my lowest moment, then saw me go on to find great happiness.

brian foster

I remember the exact moment I heard Carl Kasell's voice. I was about 20 years old and was driving through Rock Creek Park in Washington, DC. I was so taken by his voice. After that, I tuned in every hour to hear his newscasts. I just had to listen to Carl. This was years before I met him or introduced him to my mother.

Puppets are the reason that Carl Kasell is my stepfather. When I was in second grade, an amazing teacher by the name of Michael Cotter of Blue Sky Productions empowered us to work with all aspects of puppets. We learned to work with reel-to-reel tape recorders, mark cues for sound, and build puppets. In second grade!

That was pretty much the extent of my puppetry for 15 years. I had graduated from the University of Maryland with a psychology degree when, one day, my mom mentioned that Michael Cotter was doing a show at the Unitarian Church. She suggested I go check him out. I had butterflies meeting him again, as though I was back in second grade. I went backstage and said, "Remember me? I was your star puppeteer." He didn't, but mentioned that if I wanted a job, to come to an audition. I got the job and worked intensely with him for about three years. We did a show a day, 350 shows a year. Then I formed my own company and needed some puppets.

This is where Carl Kasell re-entered the picture. My mom happened to be driving through Wheaton, Maryland, and noticed some great looking puppets in a magic shop window. I checked it out and it turned out, that the puppet maker was Barry Gordemer, who also worked at NPR. One of the first questions I asked him was, "Do you know Carl Kasell?"

He said, "Yes, I work with him every day." And Barry took me on a tour of NPR. I was a little awestruck by the NPR organization and meeting Carl Kasell! I could see why people get nervous when they're around him and break out in a sweat. Barry told me later that Carl's wife had passed away, which prompted me to suggest to Barry that maybe Carl Kasell could marry my mom. (I had a history of asking men to marry my mom, including my doctor when I was a boy. My parents separated when I was three, and as an only son, I really wanted to see her get married again. I took it upon myself to make sure she wasn't alone.)

Three years went by, and Barry invited me to dinner with Carl. We went to a casual Italian restaurant, and I was a little speechless. I was having dinner with Carl Kasell! I bragged about it to all my friends. After dinner, I brought up marriage again to Barry, "Hey maybe we should hook my mom and Carl up now. It's been a few years."

He said, "Yeah, let's think about it," and the subject was dropped.

Carl seemed like such a nice guy, and I thought he would be a great suitor for my mom. My mom is very charming, and I was hoping for the best. It was time. I hadn't given up hope. After my doctor and a few others didn't work out, I thought Carl was the next in line.

There's some lack of clarity among the parties involved, but I'm certain that I introduced my mom and Carl. When Barry and Amy were getting married at the London Zoo, we were getting ready at the Monkey House. At some point my mom was coming toward me from one direction and Carl was coming from another direction. And I remember saying, "Hey Mom, this is Carl Kasell," and, "Carl, this is my mom." And to my recollection, that is the beginning of when they started to talk.

Carl was so suave and debonair, and he has that voice of God. How could you not like him? He has a gentle vibe. When they started dating, Carl was such a gentleman and very romantic. Every Valentine's Day the house would be full of roses. He would not only give her flowers on their wedding anniversary, but also on the anniversary of the day he proposed. I was so touched by it.

I asked him once when they were dating if he was having a good time going out with my mom. He said, "Oh yes, your mom is a real catch!"

This was a big shift for my mom, and for me. As an only son, she depended on me for many things, like taking care of the dogs and mowing the lawn. I was over there a lot. After they started dating, Carl took over many of the responsibilities. In addition to wanting a partner for my mom, I also wanted a dad. Mine had died when I was a teenager, and even though I was in my mid-thirties, Carl made me feel like I was his second son. It wouldn't have taken much to please me, but he treated me as a son in the way he cared for me.

Examples? When I was in music school and had a recital, Carl came to see the performance. He shook my hand afterward and said, "Good job." It meant so much.

One afternoon I was driving over to see them in my big white puppet van. A cat ran out in front of me and I hit it. I killed a neighborhood cat. And I'm a little squeamish, so I drove the few blocks to their house and blurted, "Oh, God. I killed a neighbor's cat!"

Carl said, "Okay, show me the cat." And he went with me to

where the cat was still lying. I was practically in tears, but he was such a man about it. He crouched down and pressed his fingers on the cat to see if it was alive. No response. So he picked it up and took care of the next steps. I felt so cared for, that he would touch the cat for me and help me.

Carl treats my mom like a queen. He is very traditional, and when he establishes a tradition, he continues it. One was to give her a new gold bracelet every Christmas. She'd flash the latest one at me and say, "Look at my new bracelet!"

"Come on, Mom," I told her, "you look like the Imelda Marcos of bracelets!" This was one of Carl's ways of showing his commitment and loyalty. My wife, Csilla, thinks their story is so romantic, meeting on a boat trip on the Thames, and going on a cruise every year on their anniversary. Carl is the god of romance!

Csilla and I and our children have just moved back to DC from Paris, where we've lived for three years. She is a physicist and was working at the Madame Curie Institute. She is Hungarian, an

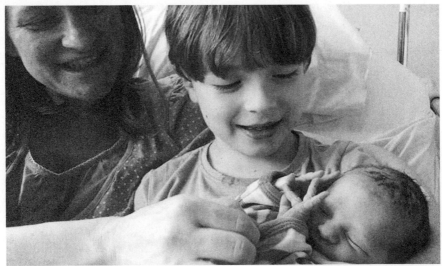

Csilla, Rocco and Lydia in a Paris hospital, 2014

EU citizen, which allowed me to work as an EU resident as well. I taught English to air traffic controllers as well as university-level courses to adults. We have a seven-year-old son named Rocco, who speaks French, Hungarian and English, and a newborn named Lydia. We're excited to be closer to Mom and Carl. He has embraced us, and we've embraced him.

With Jackie Judd and Bob Edwards in the early days of Morning Edition, *1979*

NPR

morning edition

My chair was missing. One of the last things you want to worry about when you arrive for work at 2 a.m. is where your chair went. In the early days of NPR at 1625 Eye Street, a block from the White House, we were crammed into a not-big-enough space with not enough furniture, especially chairs that weren't broken. Even after moving from Eye Street to 2025 M Street, our furniture situation wasn't what you might expect for a national news network of growing esteem. Many of our desks in the news and *Morning Edition* areas consisted of doors laid across metal filing cabinets, but they did the job.

I came to NPR as a part-time employee in 1975, anchoring newscasts on weekends. A couple of years later, I went full-time and anchored newscasts on weekday mornings. As my old friend Jim Russell explains, he was responsible for me getting the job.

After a short stint with Carl at WPIK, I joined the UPI wire and audio service and covered the war in Vietnam. In early 1971, shortly after I came back, I went to work for a brand new public radio organization with the lofty-sounding name, National Public Radio. I was one of only a few reporters working on the very first day of the program that Bill Siemering invented, All Things Considered. *It was May 3rd, which coincided with a war protest where over 20,000*

*people gathered with the intent of shutting down the govern-
ment.*

*Shortly after, when we had an opening for a newscaster,
I went after my old pal, Carl. When I called him about doing
news on ATC, our exchange went something like this:*

"All Things Considered? *Where is that?" Carl asked.*

"It's at NPR," I said.

"What's NPR?" he asked.

*So, yes, I can say that I am responsible for bringing the
legendary newscaster to NPR. By the way, Carl was not
initially embraced by all of the mostly young staff at NPR.
Many of them, in their mid-twenties, thought Carl, in his
thirties, was too old and too ingrained in the old ways of
broadcasting. That was part of NPR's mission: to sound like
America sounded. It would not have reporters and anchors
who sounded unnatural. There would be no stentorian, ar-
tificial-for-the-sake-of-authority voices on NPR. I was one
of many who had to unlearn what I had been taught about
being on the air. But Carl was never anything other than
Carl. He never had affectations to unlearn. I remember telling the twentysomethings that Carl would become the Rock
of Gibraltar of NPR News, that others would come and go,
but Carl would stay and become THE signature sound and
style.*

Jim Russell knew good radio. Brilliant fellow. I have a lot of
regard and respect for Jim.

When I started at NPR, there was no *Morning Edition* yet,
just top-of-the-hour newscasts. It was created because the member
stations wanted a morning news program to go with *All Things Con-*

Jean Cochran

At Morning Edition's *second anniversary party in 1981, my co-workers Jean Cochran, left, and Jackie Judd gave me a little peck.*

sidered. All right, we'll do it.

Morning Edition had a rough beginning. Management brought in people from the commercial world: executive producer, producer and even a couple of hosts to do the show. We had to do some rehearsing — you don't just decide to do a morning radio show the next day and go do it. You've got to plan, get all of the moving parts heading in the same direction, decide what you're going to put into it, how you're going to work it, and so forth. We began to do some dry runs and pretty soon, we sent out a sample to the stations.

They didn't like it.

Back to the drawing board. We tweaked it here, tweaked it there, and sent out another sample.

And again, they didn't like it. The harder we worked, the less

MOST LIKELY TO SUCCEED

Everleene Brown   Carl Kasell

From the 1952 Goldsboro High School "Gohisca" yearbook

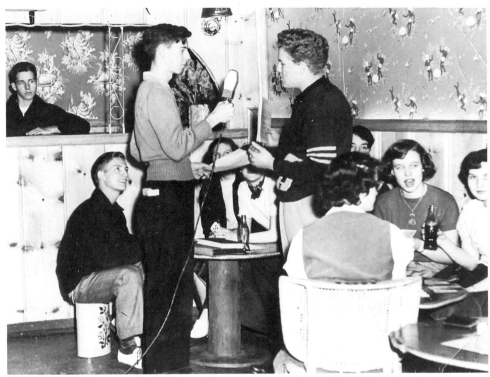

*One of my first remote broadcasts, live and direct from The Porthole,
the student lounge at Goldsboro High School*

Eighteen and ready for college   *My mother at about the same age*

*A proud member of the famed Goldsboro High School Goldmasquers drama club,
I appeared in several productions, including* Arsenic and Old Lace.

*The man who gave me my first radio job was Vassie Balkcum, owner of WGBR,
and a radio pioneer in eastern North Carolina. He was a
wonderful teacher and friend. This was taken in 2005.*

Andy Griffith was a great friend and mentor in high school and beyond. He loved North Carolina and often came back to visit. ABOVE: In 1964, he dropped by to see me at WGBR Radio in Goldsboro.

Little did I know that the funny faces, noises and voices I was making for my six-month-old son, Joe, in 1961, would someday entertain and amuse millions on Wait Wait...Don't Tell Me!

We love our dogs! ABOVE: *Mary Ann and I with Gilda in February, 2003*
BELOW: *Mary Ann with Sophie, sitting, and Gilda*

*Enjoying a crisp autumn day at our vacation home
in Warm Springs, Virginia*

*We went on a Potomac
River cruise in 2003. It is
where I asked Mary Ann
to marry me.*

Our wedding party, LEFT TO RIGHT: Adam Felber, Barry Gordemer, Sandy Brudin, the bride, officiate Peter Sagal with his daughter Gracie, Bob Edwards, the groom, Jean Cochran, Max Cacas, Lynne Kasell with Rosie Sagal and Kathleen Kasell, Brian Foster, Joe Kasell, and David Berkebile

The newlyweds

Left: *Katiann Kasell at her First Communion, 2014*
Above: *Kathleen (Kiki) Kasell*
Below: *Daughter-in-law Csilla Szabo-Foster watches Rocco's fascination with his baby sister, Lydia.*

The Kasell and Foster families in Central Park when Wait Wait was at Carnegie Hall in 2010. LEFT TO RIGHT: *Csilla Szabo-Foster; Brian Foster; holding son Rocco, Joe Kasell, Lynne Kasell, Katiann Kasell, me, Kathleen Kasell and Mary Ann Foster*

For a baseball fan, it doesn't get much better than throwing out a first pitch. I was honored to do it twice: for the St. Louis Cardinals, and, ABOVE, the Cincinnati Reds.

Another great joy of my life is magic, and NPR colleague Barry Gordemer was my mentor. No animals were harmed in the performance of our act, "Magic Edition."

The Morning Edition *team, around 1984. I'm seated in the middle behind the IBM Selectric.*
Top row: *Steve Munro, Thurston Briscoe, Sean Collins, Alice Winkler; Fred Wasser; Rod Abid*
Seated on bookshelf: *Tom McCarthy; Barry Gordemer;* standing far right: *Max Cacas*
Second row: *Bob Edwards, Audrey Wynn, Bob Ferrante, Jean Cochran, Michael Carrese, unknown, unknown;*
Front row: *Vicky O'Hara, Diane James, Taki Telonidis, Ellen McDonnell, Marie Dilg*

Photo by Paula Darte

With me at NPR's 25th anniversary party in 1995, LEFT TO RIGHT, *Ray Magliozzi, Ray Suarez, Terry Gross, Tom Magliozzi, Susan Stamberg and Bob Edwards*

BELOW: *Among my most treasured possessions are the cufflinks that President Obama gave me.*

John O'Hara

With Bob Edwards in his NPR office, early 2000s

BELOW: *At 10:55 a.m. on December 30, 2009, just before my final top-of-the-hour newscast on NPR, my longtime* Morning Edition *newscast pal and co-anchor, Jean Cochran, wishes me well.*

NPR/David Gilkey

Two men who changed my life: ABOVE, *the brilliant creator of* Wait Wait, *Doug Berman, and* BELOW, *celebrating my wedding with a cigar, is the incredibly gifted and generous* Wait Wait *host, Peter Sagal.*

CLOCKWISE FROM TOP LEFT: *The award; Bob Edwards presenting my HOF honor; my acceptance speech; my son, Joe, Mary Ann and me; signing my wall plaque (graffitti is encouraged)*

HOF photos by Donald Pointer

they liked it.

We were approaching the deadline of November 5th, 1979, very quickly, and I went home one Friday afternoon wondering if we were ever going to come up with a show to the liking of the member stations.

The next morning in the *Washington Post,* I found out that most of the staff, the outsiders, had been fired. Management decided to clean house and go inside. Jay Kernis, who had been producing other programs on NPR, was made producer, and some *ATC* folks were added, including Bob Edwards, who was "borrowed" for a short time. Bob stayed on *Morning Edition* for almost 25 years.

As for the fired hosts — I call them the "original" hosts of *Morning Edition* — it turns out we may have done at least one of them a favor. That happens; a disappointment leads to a success. Mary Tillotson went on to have a long career as reporter and anchor at CNN. Pete Williams left DC and went back to Wyoming, where he got a job as the press secretary for a congressman named Dick Cheney. And he came back to Washington with Cheney when he became the Defense Secretary under Bush Number One. And from that, of course, he went on to become a TV reporter on NBC for a number of years. Some years later, I saw Pete at an event in Washington and he introduced me to a friend. "This is Carl Kasell. He and I worked together at NPR for about 15 minutes back in 1979."

Our first big story on *Morning Edition* was the Iran Hostage Crisis, the takeover of the U.S. Embassy in Tehran. It began a day before we started *Morning Edition* and lasted for 444 days before Iran released the U.S. hostages. Interestingly, some of those hostages came to NPR and visited our tape library to listen to our coverage of the story.

For the first few years of *Morning Edition*, Jackie Judd did the top-of-the-hour news, and I did the bottom-of-the-hour news. After she left for CBS, I moved to the top-of-the-hour and Jean Cochran took my spot. My first newscast was at six in the morning, which meant setting my alarm for 1:05 a.m.

After showering and getting dressed, I fixed myself some breakfast and drove the half-hour or so to NPR. Along the way, I listened to the Washington, DC, all-news station, WTOP, to find out what was going on in the world. By the time I arrived at NPR at 2 a.m., I pretty much knew what the big stories of the day were going to be. I'd go over to the news desk to see what was going on. Do we have audio — reports from correspondents, or soundbites from newsmakers or eyewitnesses? Within minutes, my mind was putting together that first newscast. I knew what I was going to lead with, what audio I was going to use. And it happens. I could bang out a five minute newscast in no time at all.

After my last newscast at 11 a.m., I would head for home and, most days, take a three- or four-hour nap. Then, it was family time. I'd go to Joe's games and school programs, the three of us would go to movies, we would have dinner together, and by 9 p.m. I was back in bed for another four hours. I slept a lot longer on weekends, but for 30 years, my sleep cycle consisted of two long naps. And, as my son, Joe, remembers, I had the ability to power nap regardless of what was going on around me.

My dad could drop dead asleep in minutes anywhere and get a deep sleep in the process. Sometimes, this led to some comical moments. In 1981, he and I attended a Washington Capitals/Quebec Nordiques hockey game at the old Capital Center outside of DC. In the third period, the score was close and there were about 14,000 screaming fans. When I turned to my right to see how Dad was enjoying the game, he was comfortably asleep in his seat. I just shook my head and went back to watching the game.

Another took place in 1977 when my dad, mom, and I traveled to Italy to visit with our relatives. It was our second night there but dad and I were still getting over jet lag. He and I were sharing one room while my mom and grandmother were in another. Well, an earthquake hit and my mom ran into our room to wake us up. I remember her shaking my dad and yelling, "Carl, wake up! There's an earthquake!" My dad replied, "That's great. I'm going back to sleep. See you tomorrow." He fell back asleep and I followed his lead. We slept right through it while my mom and grandmother ran out into the street. We didn't realize what had happened until the next morning when we saw the aftermath on Italian television.

There's a price to pay if you want to be the first voice that people hear in the morning. While I could plan my naps around Joe's baseball games and other activities, I almost never had breakfast with him on a weekday or drove him to school. At least he could hear me and know where I was. When Joe was in college, he decided to come to work with me. On the way to NPR, we drove by bars in Georgetown that other college students were just leaving. After a few hours of watching how I made my living, by eight or nine o'clock, the novelty had worn off and he was sound asleep, sitting upright in a chair.

Joe chose another profession with normal hours.

Jean Cochran

My final morning as newscaster for Morning Edition, *December 30, 2009.*
The ever-present UNC coffee mug contained decaf, a mandate from
my doctor because of an irregular heartbeat.

early morning edition

In 1997, Morning Edition was still beginning at 6 a.m. on
the East Coast, but a programming decision by *The Christian Science Monitor* created an opportunity for NPR and me. Peter Jablow,
NPR's Executive Vice-President and Chief Operating Officer from
1994 through 1999, begins the explanation.

The decision to start "Early Morning Edition with Carl Kasell" was essentially a real estate business decision. Real Estate in the "radio sense" that an available and potentially valuable time slot was becoming available. In 1997, The Christian Science Monitor *ended its radio news service,* Monitor Radio, *which included several hour-long news programs each day, including one from 5 a.m. to 6 a.m. Eastern time. A good number of public radio stations were broadcasting Monitor Radio, and when the decision was announced that Monitor was going out of business, we at NPR had a decision to make: Do we want to put in a claim for the 5 a.m. time slot, or let some other producer (non-NPR) develop a program for the early morning audience?*

The decision we ultimately made was that the time slot was of significant value. Even though it's 2 a.m. on the West Coast, a 5 a.m. start on the East Coast was becoming more important. Since NPR was slowly, but surely, joining the digital world, our programs already had an international presence. So, that early morning hour had the potential to become valued broadcast space for NPR attracting new listeners, adjacent to the key drive time asset of Morning Edition.

We didn't have the time or the ability to make an immediate full evolution of Morning Edition to the earlier slot, so what we decided to do was create this new show, Early Morning Edition, *with the most trusted news voice in public radio, and one of the most recognizable voices in all of radio, Carl Kasell. That way we could get NPR's member stations interested in picking up the show, lay a claim for the radio real estate, and buy some invaluable time to get Morn-*

ing Edition prepared for a potential move to an hour earlier.

Early Morning Edition consisted of whatever new developments came in overnight on the wires, rebroadcasts from the previous day's *All Things Considered*, and early morning feeds from the BBC. It took only about a month to get it on the air, and lasted about a year before NPR was able to get all of the pieces in place for Morning Edition to start at five. I enjoyed doing *Early Morning Edition* because it allowed me to spread my wings a bit. I was sorry to see it end, even though it meant getting up earlier. Instead of setting my alarm for 1:05 a.m., I set it for 11 p.m.

The longer version of *Morning Edition* grew into the most listened-to program in public radio, and the most popular of the morning news programs in America. That included commercial radio and television. We had more listeners than the <u>combined</u> viewership of *The Today Show*, *Good Morning America*, and *The CBS Morning News*.

That success made what happened in the summer of 1983 all the more baffling. Over 80 of my colleagues were fired because NPR had spent its way into a huge deficit. I don't recall the exact number, but $9 million sounds familiar. We lost about 20 people from the news division, and I didn't know how long the bloodletting would continue and whether I would be next. My morning co-anchor, Jean Cochran, and I would often go to lunch at some nearby restaurant after our shift and talk about it. Should we look around for jobs and jump before we were pushed? No. We agreed that we were staying at NPR, would keep our heads down, noses to the grindstone and hope no one noticed us as the list of layoffs was drawn up. We had our jobs to do despite the drama unfolding every day. It was a scary and sad time. We would say goodbye to colleagues, shake our heads

NPR promoted Early Morning Edition *among member stations with merchandise such as coffee cups and this cap, which I keep on a shelf in my office.*

about the tragedy of good, productive people getting fired through no fault of their own, and carry on.

One of the reasons I loved going to work every morning was that I never knew what was going to happen. And anyone who has worked in the news business has experienced slow news days: days when nothing seemed to be happening that was newsworthy, days when we joked that we were going to have to make the news up again. And then, all of a sudden, the news takes on gigantic proportions. Shouts pierce the relative quiet of the newsroom. Producers and editors hurriedly begin meeting throughout the building, phones begin ringing like crazy, outgoing calls increase, and everything we had planned is off. The *Morning Edition* lineup is tossed out. We stop re-running the show for other time zones and begin reporting on what is happening that moment. Off-duty reporters are called in, experts are contacted, government agencies are involved. As the morning goes on, we're looking at how we'll cover the story for *All Thing Considered* and beyond.

Breaking news is where radio has always shone. For decades, the immediacy of radio was unmatched. No medium could get information to its consumers as quickly. Even in today's Digital Age, I'll argue that radio remains the most reliable way of getting accurate information quickly. And fastest does not always mean most accurate. With any major, breaking story, there are rumors that show up on the Internet or social media that are untrue. During 9/11, there was one moment amid the chaos when we received word that the State Department in Washington had been bombed. CBS News went on the air with the report that a car bomb had exploded outside the State Department. We could not confirm it, so we did not go with it. The report turned out to be false, and CBS had to go on the air and retract the report. Any time a story would break, we would not go with the first report on it. We would wait for confirmation, and that attention to accuracy has saved us from being burned several times.

In the early years of NPR, that tendency to wait on reporting a breaking news story was created by necessity. We didn't have the resources to cover breaking stories, so instead of being the best at reporting it, we became the best at analyzing — often the next day — what happened and putting it into perspective. Our ability to do that, and do it well, attracted an audience, and as our reputation grew, it remained the reason that people turned to NPR, even as our ability to cover breaking news increased.

The following are just a handful of the more memorable news stories we reported on at NPR, including unfathomable events that shook us all.

pope john paul II

On May 13, 1981, I had already gone home when I heard about the attempted assassination of Pope John Paul II. As an example of our limited resources, I drove back to work to help cover the story and stayed around through *All Things Considered* to report on what we knew.

the challenger space shuttle

In the late morning of January 28, 1986, I was preparing to go home after my *Morning Edition* shift. I put on my coat and picked up my briefcase and was watching the Challenger Space Shuttle launch on television. This was the 25th launch of a space shuttle, and they'd become so routinely flawless that many news organizations had stopped covering them live. When I saw the shuttle break apart 73 seconds later, I put down my briefcase, took off my coat and went back to work. Back then, we had wire machines, not computers. Just rip the copy off the machine, underline what you want to use, and get on the air with it.

the berlin wall

In late 1989, we had the fall of the Berlin Wall, which we were following very closely as it seemed the Eastern Bloc was falling, country by country, day by day. I was told that one of the reasons for the fall of communism was American television. People behind the Iron Curtain were fascinated with "Dallas." As it appeared we were getting close to the fall of East Berlin, I was talking with my colleague Jean Cochran one day and said, "When do you think the Berlin Wall will fall?"

She said, "I bet it falls today."

I said, "No, I think it'll be another week or so."

"No," she insisted. "It'll be today."

I went home. By the time I got there, Jean was on the phone.

"Guess what, Carl?" The wall had fallen.

A few years earlier, I had visited Berlin. A friend from high school had been an exchange student and spent his senior year with us in Goldsboro before going back to Germany. We visited him, and as we stood on a building in West Berlin, looking into East Berlin, I was stunned by how stark it looked. It was dull, colorless, awful. I could see where land mines had been set, and patrolling the wall were a couple of East German soldiers on bikes with submachine guns strapped to their backs. Not to keep us out, but to keep their people in. That was sad to see.

the oklahoma city bombing

Then there was April 19, 1995. Just one minute into my ten o'clock Eastern time newscast, a truck parked outside the Alfred P. Murrah Building in Oklahoma City exploded. One hundred sixty-eight people were killed: 19 of them children. That someone, a domestic terrorist as we learned later, would do something of that magnitude shocked the nation, including us in the newsroom.

There was a brief moment for each of us when we just stared in stunned silence, almost disbelief, as we read what was coming in on the wire. How an American citizen could have such hatred toward his own nation was beyond us, perhaps contributing to what was a regrettable moment for the media. Many organizations, including some of the most respected news outlets in the country, reported in the early going that the bombing was the work of Middle East extremists.

9/11

On September 11, 2001, with just over 15 minutes to go before my next top-of-the-hour newscast at nine o'clock, I left the newsroom to get my coffee mug refilled, not knowing that in a little over a minute, the course of American history was going to change. At 8:46 and 26 seconds, American Airlines Flight 11 smashed into the north side of the north tower of the World Trade Center in New York. I walked back into the newsroom with my coffee moments later and saw the video of the smoke pouring from the tower. It reminded me of a moment in my childhood, in the summer between fifth and sixth grades, when an Army Air Force B-25 bomber crashed into the Empire State Building. That happened on an overcast, foggy day and the pilot had become disoriented as he was trying to land at the Newark airport. But this crash happened on a bright, sunny day.

We had little to go on when I went into the booth to do my newscast, only a couple of sentences about what we knew at that point, which was that a plane had crashed into the building. During my newscast, at 9:03 a.m., I saw a bulletin on my computer monitor that a second plane had hit the other tower. It was then that I was beginning to think, something's not right here. Then, at 9:37, an American Airlines flight hit the Pentagon. And at 9:59, the south tower of the World Trade Center collapsed, plummeting to the street below. Four minutes later, United Flight 93 went down in a Pennsylvania field. At 10:28, the north tower collapsed.

Things were happening so quickly that it was useless to try to put together a newscast for the top of the hour. Anything I wrote would be immediately outdated. There was a lot of ad-libbing.

We were trying our best to gather audio of any type to use. We made calls to interview the eyewitnesses, which was a rarity for us in the newscast unit. Normally, the interviews were done by the hosts, like Bob, Susan, Nina and Linda. That day, the news was moving so fast, we all did whatever had to be done to get information on the air.

I was putting newscasts together on the fly, keeping an eye on what the wire services were providing. I underlined what was up to date and what I wanted to include in the next newscast. I was able to insert audio as we got it. Our people were frantically trying to find out other information such as: What about casualties? Who is responsible? Was it a coordinated effort? What is our military doing? Can we expect further attacks? Is there word from the White House? Where's the president?

Before noon, all government workers were sent home, which in downtown Washington was just about everyone. As I looked out the window, I could see all these people in the streets, like a scene from a 1950s science fiction movie like *Godzilla*, people escaping. Panic had set in. As I maintained a calm demeanor on the air, I couldn't help but look out the windows nervously, wondering what was next. Would there be more planes targeting DC?

Later, it took me about an hour to get home, a trip that usually took ten to fifteen minutes. The streets were filled with cars and people, all trying to process what had happened and fearing the unknown. It's one of those days that none of us will forget, and we'll always remember where we were when it happened.

People often ask me if I got caught up in the emotion of the story, such as with 9/11. The answer is, I didn't have time. I was too involved in planning what I needed to do next, and what information and audio was available. And I owed it to the listener to present information as straightforwardly as possible. Any feelings were pushed to the back and had to wait until I got home, where I could react just like anyone else. During 9/11, I did take just a minute in the midst of the chaos to call my son, Joe, to make sure he, his wife Lynne, and baby Kathleen were okay, as well as let them know I was safe. There was still that fear of what might happen next, and I needed that connection.

While I was more matter-of-fact about tragic events and would usually just shake my head, wondering to myself why such things could happen, Joe's mother was more demonstrative. Clara would utter, in her native Italian, phrases of sadness or short prayers. She was especially distraught after learning that children were in the daycare center that was destroyed in the Oklahoma City bombing.

Joe did remind me that in the days leading up to the Nixon resignation when I was still working at WAVA, I was a bit animated around the house, causing Clara to ask me why I was so worked up. "Because he lied to us!" was my reply.

I've often been asked how I decided what news stories to put in my newscasts. Management didn't tell the news staff what to do. There were guidelines we all had to follow, such as how to

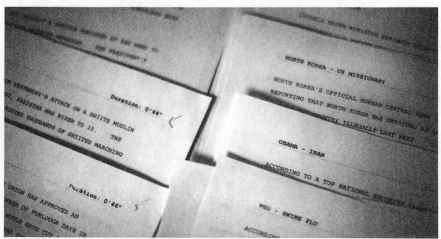

A newscast stacked and ready to read   NPR/David Gilkey

125

pronounce certain words. Even if we disagreed, we all had to pronounce the word the same for consistency. (Such as: Is Iraq pronounced eye-rack or eye-rahk? Or is it with the short "i"? Where's the accent? The official NPR pronunciation is ih-RAHK.) We had a great research department, and if a name came up that we weren't sure how to pronounce, they'd get it for us.

In the early days of my career, deciding what was important was often guided by ripping the summary of news from the AP and UPI wires. That told me what the wire editors considered the top stories to be, but as I became more experienced, I developed my own criteria for deciding what news would go into my newscasts.

The criteria for me were as follows: does it have hard news value, and is it interesting? Do your listeners — and you should know your listeners' interests — do your listeners care about this story? If you've got those qualities, you've got a good one. It's a feeling you develop over the years; when you look at a story, you

The view from my desk in the NPR newsroom   NPR/David Gilkey

know right away whether it's worthy. And among those, you know what order to stack them, and how much weight each gets. If it's an important story, I'll give it a little extra time, not the typical 30 or 45 seconds.

We didn't have newsroom computers until the mid-'80s. Before that, we had IBM Selectrics, (and before that, manual typewriters) and a production assistant would clear the wire machines every hour. They printed in triplicate, maybe it was quadruplicate, so that each of the anchors, usually Jean Cochran and I, would get a copy of what the wires were reporting. We would sort out the news by region or importance and type our stories with carbon paper so the director would have a copy, too. It was a system that worked for us, and when computers came along, some people didn't like the change. I didn't mind, and we all got used to the advantages of the word processor software. No more messy carbon paper to fuss with and no more ripping the paper out of the typewriter to start over after the story you're writing doesn't pan out.

After *Wait Wait* started recording its shows before a live audience, I anchored the news on *Morning Edition* only three days a week, Monday through Wednesday. In 2009, after 30 years of *Morning Edition*, I decided to step aside.

Do I miss it? I sure do. I loved every minute of it. There's something addictive about being on the air, knowing that the words you are choosing are providing information to the public. It's a great responsibility that I always took seriously. And there's nothing like the adrenaline rush of covering breaking news.

I had a nice run.

— milestones —

December 27, 1989

"From National Public Radio news in Washington, I'm Carl Kasell. Pictures on Romanian television today confirm that deposed president Nicolai Ceausescu and his wife Elena have been executed."

April 30, 1992

"From National Public Radio news in Washington, I'm Carl Kasell. Police in Los Angeles now say that nine people were killed in overnight rioting following the acquittal yesterday of four police officers in the beating of black motorist Rodney King."

bob edwards

The first thing every morning for 24 and a half years, Carl would come into my office just after two o'clock and sit down. Sometimes we'd just look at each other, silently wondering what we were doing there at that time of day. More often, we would talk. Vent about management. Gossip. Talk about college sports, which we both loved. It was just the way he started his day, with me, for 15 minutes every day. It was routine; it never failed. He needed that connection before he started his day. So did I. We were mutually supportive, and that was so important to my time there.

Carl is universally regarded as the nicest guy anyone ever met. He didn't cuss, rant and rave, or anything like that, but you could just look in his eyes and tell when he was quietly simmering, which wasn't very often. Carl was so solid and so good that he made the rest of us sound better. And he had perfect news judgment, impeccable judgment. What stories were important, and where they were in the newscast, what order, all of that; there was none finer than Carl in determining that.

In 1983, all of us were concerned that NPR was about to fold. It was awful. We had no money for supplies and had to go across the street to CBS to borrow copy paper. There were layoffs and we lost a lot of good people, a whole gang, and entire programs were cancelled. And it came down to one payday, a Friday, and we didn't know if they were going to pay us. But there had been a midnight agreement the night before and they made the checks.

In February of 1978, I got dressed to go to work. I was still hosting *All Things Considered* then. My wife said, "Where are you going?"

"I'm going to work."

"You're not going to work today. It snowed."

Well, a little snow wasn't going to bother me. I can get through snow. I opened the door and could not see anything but white. The snow had drifted up to the top of the door. I just shut the door. Play day. Not Carl. Carl went to work. He <u>walked</u> from Alexandria, Virginia across the bridge and did the news for *All Things Considered.* I've hated him ever since.

I used to think that if you looked up "newscaster" in the dictionary, you'd see Carl's picture, but after he started doing *Wait Wait*, there was a whole different dimension of Carl Kasell magic. This man is a rock star now. It's just exciting what's happened to Carl, but that side of him has always been there, the show biz side.

Carl's late wife, Clara, was a sweet, cheerful woman who was also a great cook. She was always busy feeding us: cakes, pies, cookies, and she didn't skimp on the butter. It's a wonder that Carl didn't weigh 300 pounds.

At Carl's wedding to Mary Ann in 2003, I was honored to be asked to do a reading. I read from *The Prophet* by Kahlil Gibran, and from Anne Morrow Lindberg's *Gift from the Sea.*

The guy was such a brick. You could always count on him. Carl would offer great empathy if you were hurting. He would listen; he would try to console you and make you feel better.

We were buddies. We were teammates. We had the same instincts, the same passion.

Carl and I also have something else in common. When each

of us was on the ballot for the National Radio Hall of Fame, we both beat out Howard Stern.

Bob Edwards is the host of The Bob Edwards Show *on Sirius XM Radio and* Bob Edwards Weekend, *distributed to public radio stations by Public Radio International (PRI). Before joining Sirius XM in 2004, Edwards hosted National Public Radio's* Morning Edition *for nearly 25 years, attracting more than 13 million listeners weekly.*

— milestones —

November 5, 1992

"From National Public Radio News in Washington, I'm Carl Kasell. President-elect Bill Clinton has already begun work leading to his inauguration on January 20th."

December 14, 2000

"From National Public Radio news in Washington, I'm Carl Kasell. Vice President Al Gore has suspended the activity of his recount committee and will address the nation tonight."

Carl Kasell sawed me in half. I don't know of any other NPR colleague who can say that. It happened at one of our staff Christmas parties. Carl and Barry Gordemer, an NPR producer/director who was Carl's mentor in magic, were going to put on a show for the kids. They were unloading their gear from their car when I walked by, and they asked if I wanted to be part of the act. Sure, why not? So, in front of dozens of wide-eyed children, Carl sawed me in half. I am not sure to this day how he did it, but it scared those little kids half to death!

On the air and around the newsroom, Carl was just a rock. He was always there, he did the job, he did it fabulously. There was no huff, no puff, no fluff; you got the news from Carl and you got it straight. He worked those incredibly awful early morning hours and he never bitched about it, ever.

When Carl started dating Mary Ann, he was much like a school kid, so happy and giggling. It was like a second life for him, which I can well understand since my husband died and I remarried, also.

Carl was always such a straight guy, it never occurred to me he would be a straight guy in the literal and comedic sense and that he would move so seamlessly from news to a show that's all about comedy and ridiculousness. And that he would he so good on *Wait Wait*! He was fabulous at it.

Women love Carl — he is a chick magnet — and I can tell you why: He's always interested in you and what you have to say. He'll always give you a big hug, a bear hug, but you're never threatened, he's not a lech!

Another thing that stands out about Carl is that he was always so unflappable. It didn't matter what would go wrong when he was on the air, whether a reporter wasn't on the line for some reason, maybe the line went down, or the copy didn't show up, or an event was happening at that very moment, it didn't matter. Carl was completely calm and collected, and he set the tone for everybody else, which is a great thing in an often chaotic newsroom.

Nina Totenberg is NPR's award-winning legal affairs correspondent. Her reports air regularly on NPR's critically acclaimed newsmagazines All Things Considered, Morning Edition, *and* Weekend Edition.

jean cochran

When I arrived at NPR in May of 1981, Carl shared the morning newscasting job with Jackie Judd. She was doing the top-of- the-hour and Carl was the bottom-of-the-hour newscaster. When Jackie was picked up by CBS, Carl moved to the top-of-the-hour news, and a succession of people did the bottom-of-the-hour until I started doing it regularly in 1989.

For the better part of 30 years, Carl would arrive at NPR each morning at two o'clock, and I'd get there somewhere around three. We went to what we called the news "ready room," where you could read the wires, open your eyes, have some coffee, read your e-mail or whatever. We'd have our coffee together and go through the wires together. There were times when no words passed between us, and then, more often than not, we would chat about what was going on at NPR, we'd kvetch, we'd complain about work, about the state of the world, about politics, about our personal lives, although Carl never was much of a complainer. There were times that I'd be ready to march into the boss's office in righteous indignation, but not Carl. He wasn't going to go there. It just wasn't in his persona to make waves or be complaining at all. That came through on the air, too, and that's one of the reasons he's one of the most beloved figures at NPR and with NPR listeners.

Carl was what, today, we would call my work husband. I have been single all my life; I kind of devoted my life to NPR. Carl had his wife, Clara, and his son, Joe. But I had what Clara didn't have. I had that morning coffee and newspaper chat at the start of the day with Carl. Clara was a sweet, kind, gentle woman, and a wonderful cook. They were a great couple, and after Clara died, Carl was lost for a while. Many of us at NPR tried to occupy his time; he and I went out to eat a time or two and went to see *Phantom of the Opera.* We were all very happy when he met Mary Ann.

There was never any danger of Carl being alone for long. He was, as Nina said in her chapter, a chick magnet! Women were traipsing through the newsroom all the time to see him. There would be reporters coming in from foreign posts who had to stop by and get their hug and kiss from Carl. He just had that knack for making you feel special.

Each morning around four, we would migrate down the hall to the newsroom where the action took place, where the newscasts were produced. The producer and editor were there, and the overnight newscaster was just leaving as we moved in. In those early hours, we worked in relative peace and quiet without having a lot of chiefs around telling us what to do. We were free to pick our own stories. We were our own editors. As newscasters, we had a lot of autonomy. Sometimes newscasters today ask producers and editors, "What should I lead with? What should I do?" Carl and I would never have thought to ask that. That's our job, that's what we do. We decide our story lineup. We decide what to lead with. That editorial judgment is what brought a little of our own character into the news.

NPR was a lot of fun in the early years because it was a much smaller organization than it is now. Frank Mankiewicz, who was our president when I came in '81, used to say, "NPR is the best kept secret in broadcasting." We were still making a name for ourselves and had about a quarter of the member stations NPR does now. There was not a lot of administrative hierarchy; there was a lot of freedom and creativity. Reporters and others were not there for the pay, because the pay was not that good. There was a lot of idealism. You were coming off the heydays of the sixties, and the civil rights movement and feminism, which carried forward into the seventies. Also, after Watergate, there was a feeling that you could make a difference with journalism. It seemed like a noble profession, and I still believe it is.

There weren't many women on the air in radio or television at that time, and NPR seemed to be on a mission to break that barrier. We had the "founding mothers of NPR": Susan Stamberg, Linda Wertheimer, Cokie Roberts and Nina Totenberg, all of whom I hold in such high esteem. I, and other women, came along later, but we were a wave that was pushing forward and we weren't going to let anything stand in our way.

Carl, right off the bat, was welcoming and accepting. I wrote some copy for him, and while at that time I wasn't the best of writers, he never complained. He always read it with authority and made it sound good. Carl was generous with his news knowledge; he never made you feel inferior. He was really an enabler in the best way because he made you feel like, "You can do this, it's not a problem." It was my first time on the national news stage, and he made me feel like I could do it.

There's a popular stereotype of the seasoned newsman: He's profane and a hard drinker, a cynical, grizzled character. Carl was the antithesis of this. The closest Carl ever got to profanity was saying, "Well, heck fire!" It was so sweet.

Carl rarely made mistakes, and the techs loved him for that reason. The man never busted a post (went past the point in the newscast for local stations to break away). The five-minute news-

David Henderson www.boomercafe.com

Jean Cochran on the air at NPR in 2013

cast is kind of the haiku of news in that there's a post at three minutes, and then you go on and do the back two minutes, which some stations cover up with local programming, but you have to hit that post at three minutes into the newscast, say, "This is NPR," take a pause, and then continue for two minutes. At the top of the hour, the news began at one minute after, the break was at four minutes after, then the back end finished at six after. Carl was rock steady. He was sure, he was reliable, and that's what you want in a news person. Really, it all adds up to trust, and Carl is trustworthy.

When Carl retired from the newscasts, I cried. Here he had been my partner for all these years, and I was losing my main ally and compatriot and stalwart colleague. There had been so many personnel changes in the evolution of the newscast unit all those years, but he and I were the constant. And he left me alone! It was quite a blow, and I was a mess.

It was no surprise that Carl did so well with *Wait Wait*. He had a flare for showmanship and would often do magic shows with Barry Gordemer. Any time he speaks at a member station or elsewhere, he always has a few tricks up his sleeve. The beauty of it is, he's Carl Kasell. He's the Walter Cronkite of radio, the staid voice that you can trust. And to see or hear him do something out of character is a gift. Audiences loved seeing the personal side of Carl Kasell.

I filled in for Carl a half dozen times on *Wait Wait*, and it was great fun. Once, they had me do a Barry White imitation. I still get people telling me that they just loved hearing me go, "Ooh, baby, baby!"

Jean Cochran retired from NPR on December 20, 2013 after 33 years of going to bed at 6 p.m.   *www.jeancochran.net*

— milestones —

"From NPR news in Washington, I'm Carl Kasell. Details are sketchy but it appears that a plane has crashed into the upper floors of the World Trade Center in New York City. There have been broadcast reports that a plane had struck it. CNN is quoting a witness who said it was a twin engine plane that flew right into the Trade Center. Witnesses do report hearing a huge explosion and heavy smoke can be seen billowing from the building at the moment. Other witnesses said they saw a small commuter plane crash into the building. So, it appears a plane has crashed into the upper floors of the World Trade Center in New York."

October 8, 2001

"From NPR news in Washington, I'm Carl Kasell. The Pentagon is still assessing the success of its bombing raids on targets in Afghanistan. President Bush says the raids in Afghanistan are the first step in the war against terrorism."

memories from
cokie roberts

When I arrived at NPR's M Street studios in 1977, it was a mess. We were squeezed into a tight space and we were all kids. Some of us were in our 30s, but some were younger than that, and the main thing about Carl in those days was that he was the grown-up. He absolutely put up with this group of messy young people working very hard for a broadcast operation that relatively few people had heard of. And then we all started working harder because they created something called *Morning Edition.* All of us who had been filing for one show were suddenly filing for two shows — and, by the way, not getting paid any more!

We knew, theoretically, it was the right thing to do because morning radio is the right thing to do. We didn't have any reason to believe that it would succeed other than theory. But when Carl became the *Morning Edition* newscast voice, that just made all the difference in the program. When the world started waking up to Carl's voice, it was, "Oh, okay; it's okay. The world has survived overnight because there is that reassurance letting me know." So, it was not only that he was the grown-up among all of us, but that he gave the American public the sense that a grown-up was in charge and letting them know that the world was still in one piece.

Now, what the listeners did not know until *Wait Wait...Don't Tell Me*! was how funny and how much fun he is. There was no hint of that on the air because it was very straight newscasting with highly professional writing, delivery and timing. You know, timing a newscast is really hard, and he did all of that to perfection. And it would have been totally inappropriate for the listeners to know that he was really witty and delightful. And a huge North Carolina sports fan. His success on *Wait Wait* was no surprise to us because we knew that Carl Kasell.

When Carl's wife Clara died, he was so sad. Carl had been such a loving, devoted husband, and everybody loved seeing that he was happy again after meeting Mary Ann. Their wedding was totally lovely and very funny with Peter as the officiate.

Carl is an incredibly kind person, and that was a constant through the many years we worked together. Just having him in the newsroom was reassuring to us. He is a tall, stately presence, and you always knew that Carl was looking out for you.

Cokie Roberts is a Morning Edition *contributor. At NPR she previously served as the congressional correspondent for more than 10 years. In addition to her work for NPR, Roberts is a political commentator for ABC News, providing analysis for all network news programming.*

C arl is not the type of person you'd tell a naughty joke to. He is such a gentleman, you'd actually want to behave well around him. In Carl's newsroom, everyone knew to behave because he set an example. When news broke and the rest of us were going crazy, Carl was this calm island of news professionalism.

There are people who, when they become celebrities, can become a little full of themselves. Never with Carl. Thoroughly modest, always gracious, and always himself. In a world of media personalities with big egos, how refreshing, how remarkable, to maintain that kind of balance. And in public radio, no one was bigger than Carl.

When I returned to NPR in 2001 as senior vice president for programming, I traveled the country visiting public radio stations. More often than not when a station had photographs in the lobby, there was a picture of Carl. He was — still is — one of the biggest stars in public radio.

Jay, seated, with Bob Edwards and me

Jay Kernis was a founding producer of Morning Edition, *left to produce stories for* 60 Minutes, *and returned to NPR as senior vice president for programming from 2001-2008.*
Kernis also produced programs at CNN and NBC, and is currently a producer for CBS Sunday Morning.

For the first decade that Carl was at NPR, we mostly worked on opposite ends of the clock. His newscasting day on *Morning Edition* was ending around the time my anchoring day on *All Things Considered* was beginning. He and I were friendly, smiling and saying hello in passing, but that was about it.

After I left *ATC* in 1986, I would occasionally fill in as host of *Morning Edition*. That's when I began getting to know him. Working that morning shift as an occasional visitor is completely unnatural and perfectly awful. First of all, if you don't do it regularly, you don't sleep. I would go to bed at 7 p.m. and set my alarm for 1:30 a.m., but I'd be awake most of the night, for fear I'd miss the alarm. Also, worrying about not going to sleep helped keep me up. And fear that, without any sleep, I would mess up on the air. An unforgiveable sin for hosts. Carl and the others who did it day after day were able to get in a routine of taking naps in the afternoon and going to bed at a normal time. Their bodies somehow adjusted to the hours. But the rest of us who filled in from time to time were UP all night, praying for sleep.

Once up and dressed, I drove through empty downtown Washington streets at 2:30 in the morning, heading for one of the few buildings with office lights glowing through the darkness. Feeling slightly ill and more than a little unsteady from sleeplessness, the *Morning Edition* production area seemed a perfect destination, the perfect place to be at 3 a.m. It felt like an intensive care unit — dimly lit, lots of computer and bleeping sounds. The patient was a two-hour radio program.

I would stagger into the newsroom looking for the world's strongest coffee machine, and there was Carl at his computer, working away on the morning's news. When he spotted me, he'd smile, get up, walk over, and give me a reassuring hug.

And that made it okay.

Carl's success on *Wait Wait* was no surprise to those of us in the newsroom who knew he was a ham. Off-mic, he performed magic tricks, and we learned he'd done radio drama in college. The *Morning Edition* format and the newscasting regimen must have been like a tight girdle for him. But several years before *Wait Wait,* he and I and a few other NPR people had the chance to shed our news shackles in front of a live audience, on a comedy show called *Radio Free Delmarva*. Van Williamson, who was working at an NPR member station in Salisbury, Maryland (he later joined NPR as *Morning Edition's* director), created a local radio show that was made up of skits and funny fake commercials. It was all spoof and just so goofy. For me, it was such a wonderful break from daily anchoring, and all those serious, heavy duty — and so often depressing — news stories. I could let loose and be silly as a waitress or some other character Van created. I'm sure Carl had similar motives, and to give you an idea of how much we enjoyed it, we happily drove the two hours to Easton, Maryland, where the show was moved and renamed *Radio from Downtown*. I started in 1991 or '92, and, after a few shows, recommended that Van recruit Carl. My husband Lou and I would drive out and stay the night at the Tidewater Inn, just across from the Avalon Theater in Easton. Carl and his wife Mary Ann did the same thing, but with their white Labradors, Gilda and Sophie (it was a dog-friendly hotel!). We averaged about five shows a year until Van ended *Radio from Downtown* in 2009.

One of the funniest Carl moments at the Avalon Theatre involved his reading aloud of the Taft-Hartley Act of 1947. The Act pertains to the power of labor unions and is a formal, very important but excruciatingly boring piece of federal law. Carl read it in his deeply authoritative newscaster voice, and it got the biggest laugh of the evening. I was beside myself, doubled over laughing. I don't think Carl knew how funny it was; he read it in genuine seriousness. But as he progressed, it got funnier and funnier, and Carl never broke his pace, he never laughed, he just kept on reciting the Act. It was hilarious! I think that's what made him so good on *Wait Wait*: He wasn't trying to be funny. He just was.

Carl is one of the sweetest souls on Earth. Beloved at NPR and by listeners.

Nationally renowned broadcast journalist Susan Stamberg is special correspondent for NPR. Stamberg is the first woman to anchor a national nightly news program and has won every major award in broadcasting. She has been inducted into the Broadcasting Hall of Fame and the Radio Hall of Fame. An NPR "founding mother," Stamberg has been on staff since the network began in 1971.

Cheryl Nemazie/Van Williamson

Performing a Radio From Downtown *sketch, with*
Susan Stamberg and Van Williamson to my left

— eight —

pluckin' on the chicks

Imagine, if you can, Susan Stamberg and me on stage before a live audience, doing a Rockettes-like dance number to the accompaniment of an accordion. Or Susan reading a commercial for a restaurant called the International House of Muskrat. Or me, "singing" a blues song about the woes of being a chicken plucker. As Susan mentioned in the previous chapter, many years before *Wait Wait...Don't Tell Me!* was hatched, she and I were dabbling in the performing arts in a similarly ridiculous manner. In 1993, Susan got me to go out to Salisbury, Maryland, on the Delmarva Peninsula, a two-and-a-half hour drive from DC, to be part of *Radio Free Delmarva*. It was a comedy sketch show that was recorded in front of a live audience for the local public radio station. The brains behind *Radio Free Delmarva* belonged to creator/producer/writer/musician/actor Van Williamson, who takes us back to those thrilling days of yesteryear.

Years before I became Carl's newscast director at NPR, I was a news producer at a public radio station in Salisbury, WSCL. It had a sort of folk, blues, jazz show on Saturday nights, and they had volunteers from the community doing the two-hour show. One week, somebody dropped out and they asked me if I wanted to do it, not as part of my regular job, but as a volunteer. I'm a musician, and have been one for most of my life, so I was just going to go in there and play some jazz discs and talk about them. After one Saturday night of doing that, I immediately realized it would be way more fun to have some of my friends come in and play live music and mix it up with the discs. I did that once with three or four friends of mine and decided to do the whole show live, and sort of made it up as we went along. At one point, we started doing some shtick in between songs. It was completely unstructured, but a friend of mine, Jack Purdy, and I started writing out some skits and began using sound effects, live and pre-recorded, and we moved the show from the studio into an auditorium. More and more people started coming to watch the show, which at that time we called Radio Free Delmarva. We had an engineer, a technical director named Jim Smith, who had worked at NPR. The show started to become a lot of fun, and we'd have guest musicians come in and guests who we interviewed. There were some skits, a radio play in a couple of acts or whatever. About a year or so into doing RFD, maybe in 1991, Jim said, "Why don't you have somebody from NPR come down here and be one of the actors?"

"Sure. How?" I asked.

He said, "Well, I know some people there. Who do you want?"

"How about Susan Stamberg?" She was the most prominent broadcaster I could think of, and I was a huge fan of her work over the years. Might as well aim high.

Jim said, "Okay."

The next thing I knew, Susan was coming down for the next show. Jack and I wrote her a nice, fat part, and we had

Cheryl Nemazie/Van Williamson

ABOVE: Radio From Downtown *on stage at the Avalon Theater*
in Easton, Maryland, mid-'90s
BELOW: *To my left, Susan Stamberg, Van Williamson and Jack Purdy*

Cheryl Nemazie/Van Williamson

maybe four or five actors and a five-piece band. Susan loved it and said, "Any time you want to write a part for me, I'll come down." I was over the moon, totally.

After Susan came down a few times, she said, "You know who would really love this is Carl Kasell."

Jack and I wrote a part for him; as I recall, it was the announcer part that we wrote, the straight guy. He'd announce the set-ups to the acts, and I'd give him silly things to read between acts. The plays got more and more complicated with 20 or more parts, and I only had four or five actors, but Carl would always play the announcer, because, well, he was Carl Kasell! What would be better than to have him be him?

When I left WSCL and went to work at NPR, we moved the show from Salisbury to Easton, Maryland, which was still an hour and a half drive for them. We moved into an historic theater, the Avalon, a fabulous restored Art Deco theater in downtown Easton, and we changed the name to Radio From Downtown. *Susan and Lou, and Carl and Mary Ann would come down and stay, and we would all*

Cheryl Nemazie/Van Williamson

Susan awaits her cue while I examine my next line during a Radio From Downtown *show in the mid-'90s.*

have just the grandest time. This was a show that had essentially zero rehearsal, except for one run-through at the table the afternoon of the show. At this point, the show consisted of 20-25 people including the crew, and it was impossible to get everybody together the day before the show to rehearse. The acts and skits and fake commercials got more and more complicated and crazed. I would write Carl into nearly all of the fake commercials, and one of my favorite things was to have Susan and Carl do a fake commercial for some highly ridiculous, made-up product. They would give it their all, and these people were really great professionals and so much fun to work with. Carl carried his straight-man thing, I mean, it's his personality, and whatever it was, even the most outlandish parts I gave him, he just did them flaw-

lessly in that Carl Kasell voice and style that NPR listeners were so familiar with.

Greg Smith, a former editor at NPR who started working on RFD as a writer and actor, wrote a song with me. It was a blues song that had to do with chickens. Well, Carl is not a singer, he'd be the first to tell you, so we had the band play what was essentially a 12-bar blues, and Carl did it as a talking blues. About chickens. Here are the lyrics, and remember: These words came out of legendary broadcaster Carl Kasell's mouth!

The Chicken Song (Pluckin' on the Chicks)

When I was a young man living out in the sticks,
My daddy said, "There's money, son, in pluckin' them chicks."
I said, "No Daddy, no. It don't feel right.
I'd rather pluck this here guitar and stay out all night."

Cuz in all kinds of weather,
You're pluckin' on the feathers;
Pluckin' on the chicks.

But my daddy told me, "Now listen here, boy,
That guitar you got there ain't nothin but a toy.
You want to make some real scratch, listen what I say.
Put your trust in chickens, which I'm doing to this day."

So in all kinds of weather,
I'm pluckin' on the feathers.
I'm pluckin' on the chicks,
I'm pluckin' away ... I'm pluckin' away ...

That was really skin-of-your-teeth radio, and there was no way of knowing whether any of this stuff would actually come off in front of an audience. (In fact, that was probably part of the appeal for the audience, that the skits would not go as planned.) I was on the stage because I was one of the actors, and when it was Carl's turn to go, I'd point to him, and he'd start reading these absurd lyrics. The combination of that commanding voice of authority and credibility reading lyrics about chickens was a scream!

Another time, we were doing a spoof on the Super Bowl. At the end of each game, the winning quarterback or whoever would look into the camera and say, "I'm going to Disneyland!" Our version went, "I'm going to The Hague!" And then Carl would come on and do 30 to 45 seconds about The Hague, the international court in the Netherlands. The information was legit, but Carl read it as if it was a commercial and it was very funny, one of my favorites.

Susan and Carl got to ham it up in a way they wouldn't be doing on NPR. Radio From Downtown *was loose, and although there was a script, the actors could have their way with it, and they did. That was the beauty of it, really. I would write the stuff, but what Susan, Carl and the other actors came up with was way funnier and way more interesting. It was a total thrill for me to hear something that I wrote coming out of the mouth of Carl Kasell, or Susan Stamberg, or Jean Cochran, who was on the show a few times, too.*

The last show was 2009. I'm thinking of cranking it up again. Carl and Susan did the show for at least 10 years, maybe 12. It required a commitment that only somebody who loves the beauty of improvised radio could give.

*Just a few more things about Carl. When Barry Gorde-
mer, the* Morning Edition *director, left to work in another
area, I was given his job and stayed as director for about
12 years. Here's how good Carl was. It really didn't matter
what I was doing in the control room, Carl's newscast would
be great whether I was in there or not. So I would do things
to make it appear that I was actually directing Carl, even
though he was on autopilot. The only thing I really had to do
was make sure his microphone was open at the right times.
The other tech people and I fooled ourselves into thinking
that we were really directing Carl's newscasts, but we really
didn't matter.*

Van is a talented musician and writer, and those shows at
Radio From Downtown were great fun. I hope he starts it up again.
He knows where to find me.

RFD wasn't the only live radio silliness I did before *Wait
Wait*. In 1994, I was invited to Overland Park, Kansas, to take part in
a show put on by *Imagination Workshop,* a live radio comedy troupe
that spoofs politics, celebrities, sports figures, etc. on Kansas public
radio stations. The group is now known as *Right Between the Ears*.

It was their 10th anniversary and the show was broadcast on
NPR. Just as with *Radio from Downtown* and *Wait Wait*, I appeared
as myself in several sketches, including one promoting a beer designed for people who were choking on their food. Here is part of
the script, which was accompanied by various guttural sound effects:

*Yes, the cold distinctive taste of Heimlich brings up the
best in everyone. The Heimlich brewmasters could spend a*

Right Between the Ears

Performing a phony beer commercial on stage near Kansas City with Rick Tamblyn, a member of Right Between the Ears *comedy sketch cast*

lot of time and money on things like imported hops, pure artesian water and scientific brewing methods, then pass the cost on to you. But they figure, hey, why waste all that energy on a beer that's going to wind up in your shoes anyway? Heimlich's no gag. See for yourself. Just grab a longneck and dislodge your thirst today. Your friends will gasp in appreciation. Heimlich, the beer people really get choked up for.

We did that show before a sold-out crowd at Yardley Hall in Overland Park. I had a great time with a very funny and talented group of actors. All these years later, *Right Between the Ears* is still going strong. So am I, and I hope to make it back for an encore.

NPR/Nelson Hsu

When Wait Wait...Don't Tell Me! *was being developed,*
the creators needed a serious journalist with class
and dignity to add balance to the show.
Clearly, I was the right choice.

wait wait!

Doug Berman was in the audience at a 1997 meeting of public radio program directors in Boston. A number of NPR on-air personalities were there and one evening, I was asked to preside at a session and introduce the NPR glitterati. I did, and I cracked a few jokes. The various NPR stars took questions, and toward the end of the program, someone in the audience asked, "What about you, Carl, why don't you tell us something about you?"

"Sure," I said, "What do you want to know?"

"What time do you get up each morning?"

"I set my alarm clock for 1:05," I replied.

"Why 1:05? Why not one o'clock?"

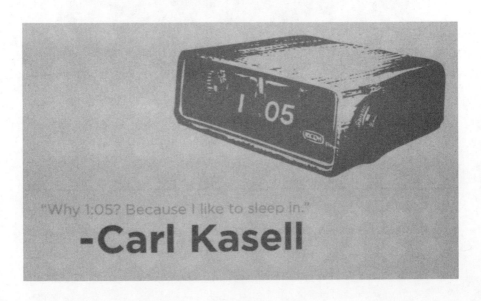

"Why 1:05? Because I like to sleep in."
-Carl Kasell

"Oh, that's just too early. I like to sleep in!" That got a nice laugh, and Doug, who'd had great success as producer of *Car Talk*, liked, and maybe was even surprised, that I had a sense of humor. That led to me being offered a chance to be on a new quiz program he was developing called, *Wait Wait...Don't Tell Me!*

But, as Doug explains, that wasn't our first encounter:

I first met Carl in 1982, when I was a lowly college kid working on All Things Considered. *I was completely intimidated by being at NPR, seeing the people I considered "stars" doing normal human things like walking, talking and typing. And having faces.*

I was making copies in the newsroom one day when I heard a voice I instantly recognized. After debating whether I should even bother the guy, I nervously went over to Mr. Kasell, introduced myself, and told him it was an honor to meet him. I was prepared to quickly back away with my eyes on the floor.

Instead, Carl shook my hand and held it while he looked me right in the eye with real interest. He told me it was great to have me at NPR. Carl asked me about myself and how I'd arrived at NPR. He shared some stories of his early days in the business. After five minutes or so of delightful conversation, he apologized and said he had to go do a newscast, wished me lots of luck and said he sure hoped he'd see me around. His warmth and kindness were genuine and, as I was to learn over the years, he shared them with pretty much everybody he ever met.

The *Wait Wait* story, though, began about a year before Doug

Melody Kramer

*The Chase Bank Auditorium in Chicago, which holds over 500
people, is where* Wait Wait *is recorded most Thursday nights.
This was on September 18, 2008 when Leonard Nimoy,
seated below the big sign, was the guest.*

saw me at the program directors' conference. There had been discussion within NPR about developing a news quiz program. Murray Horwitz, who was director of Jazz, Classical Music, and Entertainment Programming at NPR, refined the idea for a show that, when Doug became involved, eventually became the *Wait Wait* you hear today.

Murray and I became good friends after he joined NPR in 1989, partly because we shared a love of radio drama and acting. He is an incredibly gifted actor, writer, director and producer, and won multiple awards, including a Tony, an Emmy and a Grammy for the Broadway musical, "Ain't Misbehavin'." We both had worked for *The Lost Colony* production in North Carolina, though at different times. Murray shares some memories:

As an NPR vice president, I was able to squirrel aside enough money to hire the perfect person for the job: Doug Berman. Dougie was executive producer of Car Talk, *which had grown into a huge hit for NPR since it went national in 1987. The concept for a <u>comedy</u> news quiz that Doug came back with was, as we've watched it develop, brilliant. Using Carl was Dougie's idea, as were most of the good ideas about* Wait Wait, *and I went nuts when he called to tell me. Perfect! Great! Fabulous! I knew Carl was a performer and had a great sense of the audience and great timing. It was a marvelous idea.*

Carl's talent and integrity, not to mention those famous "pipes," had as much to do with making the show a success as anything else.

When the offer came to do *Wait Wait*, I grabbed it because that's the kind of program I grew up on and had always wanted to be on. So many of those hours I spent as a youngster listening to the radio while my mother was trying to get me to go out and play were spent spellbound by programs like *Truth or Consequences*, with Ralph Edwards, *People are Funny*, with Art Linkletter, and two shows that Bert Parks had, *Break the Bank* and *Stop the Music!* I thought, maybe one day I can do that, and, by golly, I did for 16 years. Not hosting, like those greats did; that's Peter Sagal's job. Let's say Peter was Groucho and I was his George Fenneman.

As a matter of fact, Doug said that when he was given the job of developing the program, he thought back to Groucho's *You Bet Your Life*. He said it was basically a program that they built to display Groucho's comedic talents. That's what he wanted to do with *Wait Wait*, and did, with panelists like Paula Poundstone, Mo

Jerry A. Schulman

On stage in 2009 with one of my favorite people, Peter Sagal

Rocca, Roy Blount, Jr., Roxanne Roberts, Tom Bodett, Adam Felber, Charlie Pierce, P.J. O'Rourke, Amy Dickinson, Alonzo Bodden, Faith Salie, Brian Babylon, Kyrie O'Connor and so many others; they're funny people and the quiz program is designed to display their talents.

But *Wait Wait* had to have somebody serious, too, somebody with class, somebody with dignity, so, they got me. If you've heard the program, you know how that worked out. Our unofficial slogan is "NPR without the dignity."

Doug recalls those early days of *Wait Wait:*

When I heard Carl nail that joke about getting up at 1:05 every morning, I told him I was working on this show, and asked if he would be interested.

He said, "You bet I would be!"

The only tricky part was getting the News Division to go along, because Carl was still the voice of NPR News at the top-of-the-hour. Some executives in the News Division felt it was inappropriate for NPR's foremost newscaster to be doing comedy about news. They were absolutely right, of course, but I'm glad we somehow got away with it, because no one else could have done what Carl did for Wait Wait.

No one else could have done what Doug did for my career, and, for that matter, what he did for public radio. Before *Car Talk* came along, there wasn't much to laugh at on public radio. We were quite serious, but, as Doug explains, his shows were more than just funny.

*When people ask me to define the shows I produce (*Car Talk *and* Wait Wait*), I describe them as "not a <u>complete</u> waste of time." What that means is that there's information in the shows that's actually useful and worthwhile. Not much, mind you, but once you're drawn in by something that interests you, and your brain is "distracted" by processing something useful, the humor hits you by surprise, which makes it that much more delightful.*

This is a long way of explaining why Carl was absolutely essential to Wait Wait. *In the same way that Tom and Ray's actual knowledge of how to fix cars draws you in and makes* Car Talk's *humor work, Carl represented trustworthy information to NPR listeners in a way no one else could. And by bringing that to the show every week, he made our humor 100 times better.*

At the beginning, *Wait Wait* was looking for ways to define

Jerry A. Schulman

On the rare occasions when Peter Sagal had to go to "camp,"
we had guest hosts, such as Drew Carey.

itself. It had to be a program that involved listener participation, and it had to deal with current happenings. But, how would we go about doing it? We failed miserably early on. It was a lousy program. I have a copy of it on a CD at home and I listen to it now and then. Compared to the show it became, it was terrible. Our first host, Dan Coffey, didn't last long, only about four months. It wasn't his fault. Dan was a funny guy whose comedy program, *Ask Dr. Science,* was heard on public radio stations across the country. Dan was just not what we needed for the role. He is such a nice guy, and maybe he didn't have quite enough edge.

Peter Sagal was a panelist at the time and was given a shot at being the host. Of course, it worked out great. Peter can make jokes off the top of his head, one right after another. He's very quick, very

Melody Kramer

WAIT WAIT RECEIVES A 2008 PEABODY AWARD
LEFT TO RIGHT: *Doug Berman, executive producer, me,
Peter Sagal, Rod Abid, former senior producer, Charlie Pierce, panelist,
Philipp Goedicke, limericist, Emily Ecton, former producer*

intelligent, but we were still left with trying to make the program better. When we started the show, it wasn't done in front of a live audience. I was sitting in a studio at NPR in Washington with Roxanne Roberts, Peter was in New York, and the panelists could be scattered anywhere from London to Los Angeles. I didn't meet Peter until about four months into the show. With no audience, we had to laugh at our own jokes, like the Car Guys do, although I've never heard anyone laugh the way Tom and Ray do.

We struggled to get celebrity guests to appear. They hadn't heard of us and wouldn't return our calls. So we used NPR celebrities, people like Nina Totenberg, Susan Stamberg, Cokie Roberts, Cory Flintoff, Robert Siegel, Dan Schorr and others. At the beginning of *Wait Wait*, a couple of member station managers came to me and said, "You shouldn't be doing that show. It takes away from your credibility, your dignity as a newsman." After those NPR luminaries took part in the silliness, and were very funny, I had it made.

Wait Wait slowly got better but, on occasion, when we took the show on the road, we found how much better it was with an audience. Actually, we weren't sure it was going to work the first time we tried it, in Salt Lake City in January of 2000. But it did, and over and over in city after city, people would turn out by the thousands. Not only were they willing to pay to see a free radio show, they'd stand in long lines to do so. *Wait Wait* became a hit, and celebrities began returning our calls.

As the show was being formed, the news was a bit dry. What would we talk and joke about? But then, as Peter has often said, it was like manna from heaven. First, only a few weeks after we started the show, it was Monica Lewinsky. Then Viagra. And, of course, the Bush Administration later on. It was then we realized that as long as we had governments — federal, state, local and even foreign governments — we would have material.

The reason that *Wait Wait* is based in Chicago and does most of its weekly shows at the Chase Bank Auditorium is Torey Malatia, who was general manager of WBEZ-FM, Chicago's public radio station. He was responsible for the creation of *This American Life,* and as Doug Berman remembers, was key in *Wait Wait*'s survival in the early days.

Torey was relentlessly supportive of us. And that was particularly important in the early days when the show was new and struggling to find its voice. The first three months we were on the air, we were still figuring out what the show was. At WBEZ in Chicago, Torey had put us on in place of another show that had some dedicated listeners.

One evening I decided to attend one of WBEZ's board meetings. I went incognito and sat in the back. When the subject of Wait Wait *came up, one very angry gentleman went on about how awful this new show was and that Torey should put the old show back on. Torey calmly explained that he had faith in* Wait Wait, *and it was produced by Doug Berman, who was behind the hit show* Car Talk. *The gentleman shot back, "Well, he may have a hit in* Car Talk, *but that guy's got a flop on his hands with this one!" I covered my face so Torey wouldn't see me laughing as he urged patience. Torey was a true believer from the outset, and we will be forever grateful for his support.*

One reason for *Wait Wait's* popularity is that it makes fun of the news when the news isn't much fun. Much as *The Daily Show* and *The Colbert Report* do, we serve as an outlet for the listener's frustrations. Or, as Peter has said, we say the things *on* the radio that most people just shout *at* their radio.

There was only one time our show didn't air: the weekend after 9/11. It wouldn't have been appropriate, and NPR was wall-to-wall with news coverage about the attack. But when we did go back on the air the following week, there was some discussion about "how do we do this after such a great tragedy?" After a lot of thought, we decided to do our show as we always did. The listener response was great: hundreds of e-mails saying, "Thank you, we needed a laugh. We needed a break."

When we learned in April of 2008 that *Wait Wait* had won a Peabody Award, Doug sent out a release thanking both the Clinton and Bush administrations for feeding us all the material we'd had and asked if there was some way we could do away with the term limits on presidents.

The Peabody ceremony was in New York, and we had a great time. I got to meet some really interesting people like Tina Fey, Alec Baldwin, and Stephen Colbert. And, you know, the real Stephen is not like the guy you see on *The Colbert Report*. He's a very soft-spoken and polite guy.

Just when we feared our material was drying up as the Bush presidency ended, we had the presidential campaign to play with. And of course, there were always the stupid criminals who provided fodder for our joke makers. One of my favorites was the young man who was so angry at someone that he took the time to write a note, including a threat of violence and a promise to stalk that person. He

Melody Kramer

One of my favorite parts of Wait Wait *was meeting listeners after the show. There would generally be a large group waiting for my words of wisdom.*

Melody Kramer

In September of 2007, we played before a crowd of over 10,000 at Chicago's outdoor Pritzker Pavilion in Millenium Park. It was such a great success, we did it again the next year. It poured, but a large group of die-hard Wait Wait *fans still turned out.*

Laurie Chipps

169

Melody Kramer

Leonard Nimoy was among the many big stars who joined us to play "Not My Job." He took the time to teach me how to do the "live long and prosper" Vulcan salute. If you are a dedicated Trekkie, you know that his character, Mr. Spock, first flashed it in a 1967 episode of Star Trek, *and that Nimoy based it on a Jewish blessing he saw as a child.*

put the note in an envelope, sealed it, addressed it, and put it on a table near the door along with other letters his mother was going to mail. A little later, his mom came in, looked at the envelope, and saw that her son forgot to put the return address on it. She did it for him, and he ended up serving time.

Or, how about the man who robbed a bank, ran outside waving his gun, and hijacked a car, only to find that he couldn't drive it? It had a stick shift. Before he could find another getaway vehicle with an automatic transmission, the police were there.

What's truly amazing about *Wait Wait* is the size of the staff. It's small; only four or five people. The main writer is Peter, a comedic genius. Most of the punch lines you hear from the panel and Peter are improv. The panelists don't know what's coming, which is part of the magic. Some of the show is scripted: the questions and answers, the openings and the credits, and the panelists' stories for "Bluff the Listener," and, of course, my lines and impersonations. Doug recalls the origin:

Early on, we discovered that every time we asked Carl to do an impersonation of a newsmaker, it somehow always sounded exactly like Carl Kasell. Whether it was Henry Kissinger or Britney Spears, it still sounded just like Carl reading the news. So we really embraced that, and Carl, of course, was such a good sport about it that it became a signature of the show and the basis for our opening game, "Who's Carl This Time?"

The quiz questions and answers are researched and written ahead of time by Peter and the great staff in Chicago led by Executive Producer Mike Danforth and Senior Producer Ian Chillag. They start on Monday, sifting through the news to find stories that they can make jokes about and that will fit into the show segments. When I arrived in Chicago on Thursdays, I would go to the studios of WBEZ, the NPR member station and home to *Wait Wait*. The studios are located on Navy Pier, and each time I went there, I thought of my father, who was stationed in Chicago when he was in the Navy during World War I.

At WBEZ, we would run through what Peter and the staff had written. Often, there were rewrites, and then we would go to the Chase Bank Auditorium in downtown Chicago with a full show prepared, and often do a read-through as Doug listened in on the phone. As carefully and well written as it was, a lot of the best material wound up being unplanned, thanks to the spontaneous wit of the panelists, guests, and Peter.

The audiences loved it, and one thing that surprised me was the wide range of fans, from very young people who I thought should have been home in bed by the time our taping ended, to senior citizens. And college girls seemed especially fond of the show. Here's Doug, again:

Carl became a rock star. It happened organically. It turned out that Wait Wait *listeners genuinely loved Carl even before they heard him read news-related limericks. They were waking up to him every day. His would be the first voice they'd hear. Carl would tell them that the world was still in one piece. So there was already a bond there; every listener felt Carl was already, in some way, a close, personal friend.*

And then, when they heard him on Wait Wait, *they picked up on* our *genuine affection for Carl on the show. They could tell by the role we gave him and the way we treated him that we revered him. And they also could tell that Carl was a great sport. He was willing to put his tremendous dignity on the line so that we could all have a good laugh. The fool!*

Seriously, the fact that he was so game to play along just endeared him all the more to NPR listeners. So it became a genuine love fest. And it was particularly strong among women under 30. After the shows, Peter would be surrounded by the Star Trek *nerds asking if he spoke Klingon, while all the college-aged women would be taking pictures with Carl.*

In one of our segments called "Not My Job," a celebrity would be interviewed about what was going on in their life and then would play a game based on a subject well out of their field. As we found out, a lot of famous people listened to us and wanted to be on. Through a mutual friend of Peter, we found out that Tom Hanks is a regular listener and that led to his appearance on our show. It was no surprise that Tom has a great sense of humor. It was a bit surprising to find out that *NBC Nightly News* anchor Brian Williams is such a funny guy. I believe his appearance was at Carnegie Hall.

And then there was a fellow from Chicago with an odd name who was running for the U.S. Senate. We, mostly Peter and the panel, made fun of Barack Obama's name during the 2004 campaign, and we went so far as to have a branding consultant on, who said that Mr. Obama might want to consider changing his name to something less unusual. After he won the Senate race, he wanted to come on our show to set the record straight. He appeared in the summer of 2005 to play "Not My Job." The Senator from Illinois let us know that he had been listening a year earlier and heard us making fun of his name.

One of the funniest moments came during the pre-game interview as Peter reminded Mr. Obama about his position on school graduations.

Peter: *You delivered a speech here in Illinois recently in which you came out foursquare, and somewhat provocatively, against eighth-grade graduations. Sir, my eighth-grade graduation was the high point of my life. So, what's the problem with eighth-grade graduations?*

Obama: *We're trying to prevent young people from taking your career path. We want them to do something with their lives.*

When the interview ended, Peter cued me to give the title of the "Not My Job" game that week.

"You're in the Lunatic Hall of Fame," I said, which included three questions about the superstitions of Baseball Hall-of-Famer Wade Boggs. Senator Obama got two out of three answers correct and won my voice on the answering machine of a woman named Bobbye Larson from Duluth, Minnesota. I hope she's a Democrat.

Mr. Obama had not yet announced his candidacy for president, and Peter tried to get him to do so on *Wait Wait*.

Peter: *Senator Obama, let us all know, tell the people your plans.*

Obama: *My plans are to go home and do the dishes like my wife told me to do.*

As the senator walked off stage after the show, Peter told the audience, "You know folks, there goes a guy who's going to be president one day."

And who would have expected a U.S. Supreme Court justice to be one of our "Not My Job" guests? Here's how that happened. We were doing our show in Berkeley, California, in 2006 and Linda Ronstadt was to be one of our guests. She showed up and brought a friend and the friend's husband. We were all backstage chatting, and the friend's husband and I talked for a while. He handed me his card, and I didn't really look at it, just put it in my pocket. Later, I asked him, "What do you do?"

He said, "I'm a federal judge."

I said, "Well, that's just a step away from the Supreme Court, isn't it?"

"No," he said, "that won't happen for me. My brother has already done it."

I looked at the business card, and the last name was Breyer. Charles Breyer. Supreme Court Justice Stephen Breyer's brother. As the conversation went on, we decided it would be a great idea to have his brother on the program. He, Charles, was a regular listener. He said, "I'm going to call my brother Monday morning and tell him to be on your show." He did, and the justice agreed to do it. As we heard in his interview with Peter, Justice Breyer, who's close to my age, did it for much the same reason I wanted to be on *Wait Wait*.

Peter: *I have to tell you that as soon as it was announced that you were going to be joining us to play this game, the question went up from a concerned nation, which was: Why would a man such as you ever do such a thing like this? So let me put it to you: Why — not that I'm not grateful — but why would a man like you do such a thing as this?*

Justice Breyer: *It was my sister-in-law who wanted me to do it, and I wanted peace in the family.*

Peter: *I understand.*

Justice Breyer: *I also rather like old-time radio programs. When I was a boy, I used to listen to* The Lone Ranger *and various other programs, so I have a fond recollection.*

Justice Breyer became the first sitting Supreme Court justice to appear on any quiz program of any kind. He was very funny, a trait we don't normally associate with High Court Justices.

I've been asked whether I rehearsed the impersonations I did for the opening of "Not My Job." If you've heard them, you know the answer: of course not.

"Not My Job"
June 12, 2010
Topic: World Cup soccer

Peter: *Robert Klein, we've asked you here today to play a game that we're calling:*
Carl: *Gooooooooooooooooooooooooooooooooooooooooooooooooooo oooooooooooooooooooooooooooooooooooooooooooooooooooooooooo ooooooooooooooooooooooooooooooal! (27 seconds)*

I'm often asked how *Wait Wait...Don't Tell Me!* got its name. I don't remember, but Doug does.

We were piloting the show in New York City in the mid-90s, at the Algonquin Hotel — hoping some of the high-brow history of that place would rub off on us. It most certainly didn't. But one of the panelists we auditioned was Mark Katz, who wrote jokes for Bill Clinton's speeches. He just came up to me and said he had a suggestion for the name of the the show. Mark was only half serious, but I loved it. And we never really considered anything else.

When *Wait Wait* went on the air, we didn't have much of a budget. We had no budget, really. And we were having listeners call in and play games, and we could only say, well, you're a winner. And that's it. We wanted to give them a gift or a prize. Doug ex-

It isn't Radio, it's NPR.

We provide the best news coverage you'll find anywhere in the country, and we rank right up there with the best news organizations in the world. And at the local level, NPR member stations have become essential connections between listeners and communities, even more so since local ownership of commercial stations became so rare.

Even in my hometown, the station I first worked at is owned by a company that's not based there anymore. It's in another city. But with public radio, that local connection, that local touch, is still there. Public radio has never been more important.

Jean Cochran

©Jim Borgman

Above left: *In the NPR newsroom at* Morning Edition's *second anniversary party in 1981* Above right: *Mid-1980s with editorial assistant Debra Kirsch and Bob Edwards*

Left: *To my right is Red Barber, at an NPR party honoring the broadcasting legend. His Friday morning chats with Bob Edwards from 1981-1992 were pure joy.*

Some of the funniest people in the world take the Wait Wait *stage each week. Many of them are shown* below *in an early promotional piece.*

the oddly informative news quiz

When Wait Wait *was being developed, NPR contracted with John Burke and Janice Gavan of VisABILITY, Inc. to make 700 Carl Kasell bobbleheads to send to each public radio station manager as a way of drumming up interest in the show. One recipient put his on eBay. It sold for $750.*

At many of Wait Wait's *tapings, I made my entrance by running in from the wing, across the stage, and high-fiving the panelists on my way to my podium. The crowds seemed to like it. In these photos, the panelists are, from first slap to last, Paul Provenza, Faith Salie and Tom Bodett.*

Dan Lambert, Maine Public Broadcasting

One of the biggest surprises I received on our Wait Wait *tour stops happened in Portland, Maine, where we appeared on behalf of Maine Public Broadcasting. Unbeknownst to me, everyone entering the 1,900-seat theater was given a life-sized photo of my head on a stick. Printed on the back of the photos were instructions for the audience to raise them when Peter Sagal gave the verbal cue. When he introduced me, nearly everyone lifted my face in front of theirs. Oh, Peter.*

BELOW: *Me, holding me.*

Mark Vogelzang, Maine Public Broadcasting

Wait Wait *is described as NPR's oddly informative news quiz show, and
"odd" certainly describes the throw pillow that is for sale in the
shop at NPR headquarters and at shop.npr.org.*

BELOW LEFT: *An example of what the* Wait Wait *staff does between shows*
BELOW RIGHT: *Signing a Carl Kasell Pillow after a* Wait Wait *taping.
At home, one of our dogs just stares at the pillow and growls.*

If you are one of the 3,000 + recipients of my voice on your answering machine, this is where it likely happened: a recording booth at WBEZ in Chicago.

Mackenzie Van Engelenhoven

One of my favorite things about working on Wait Wait *was how it allowed me to maintain the credibility and dignity that I worked so hard to build over the years.*

©Jerry A. Schulman

Melody Kramer

We've had a great deal of fun over the years with the NPR puppets created by our multi-talented colleague Barry Gordemer. Barry, and his company Handemonium, *have been making puppets for television, film and theatre since 1983. He created a number of puppets for NPR.*

ABOVE: *Peter Sagal and I with our likenesses.*

BELOW LEFT: *At a* Wait Wait *taping with the "Little Carl" plush doll*

©Jerry A. Schulman

ABOVE: *Comedy is serious business, or so it appears in this backstage photo with Peter Sagal and Jimmy Fallon. We appeared on Jimmy's "Late Night" show on NBC in October of 2010.*

As NPR's "Roving Ambassador," I have the pleasure of speaking at member station receptions all over the country. I enjoy meeting the people who work so hard to keep public radio alive in their local communities. ABOVE, I'm at a 2008 reception in Buffalo, New York, hosted by WBFO-FM.

The Wait Wait *crew was so kind in helping me celebrate my 80th birthday in April of 2014. Paula seems concerned, or maybe just hungry, while Roxanne appears to be shouting encouragement, or singing.*

Blockheads? WWDTM fans, and LEGO artists, Dave Kaleta and Devon Wilkop, presented Peter and me with our likenesses after a show in 2011.

With many of my Wait Wait *family at the taping of my final show on May 15, 2014.* LEFT TO RIGHT: *Ann Nguyen, CFO; Tom Bodett, panelist; Doug Berman, Benevolent Overlord; Mike Danforth, executive producer; Peter Sagal; me; Eva Wolchover, producer; Brian Babylon, panelist; Sean Kelly, intern; Emily Ecton, producer; Lorna White, technical director; and Miles Doornbos, producer*

Amy Ta

©Jerry A. Schulman

Each Wait Wait *program began when I introduced "Peeeeeeeeeter Sagal!"*

My final appearance as scorekeeper and judge was on May 15, 2014 at the Warner Theater in Washington, DC.

Amy Ta

Peter went all out for my final Chicago taping of Wait Wait *by hiring a burlesque troupe. Oh, Peter.*

Gaurav Khanna

THE SIMPSONS

DUCTION SCRIPT NO. SABF15

"PAY PAL"

SCENE 9 (CONT'D)

PETER SAGAL (V.O.)

(ON RADIO) How did the House Minority
Whip do on our news quiz, Carl Kasell?

CARL KASELL (V.O.)

(ON RADIO, ELDERLY MARBLE-MOUTH) He got
two out of three right, so he wins me,
recording his outgoing message.

Lisa and Tumi give each other a "hey, pretty cool" look.

MINORITY WHIP (V.O.)

(ON RADIO) Uh, that's okay, actually.

CARL KASELL (V.O.)

(ON RADIO, QUICKLY) It's not optional.

Lisa and Tumi CHUCKLE. We see Bart and Homer are looking
on.

BART

Who could like this show?

He turns and sees Grampa bopping happily. Homer looks at
Lisa and Tumi GIGGLING, then crosses into the master
bedroom.

INT. SIMPSON HOUSE - MASTER BEDROOM - CONTINUOUS

Homer enters happily.

HOMER

See, Marge. Problems will work
themselves out if you just leave them
alone -- like parking tickets and
global warming.

---

*Finally, we
"made it"!
But, really?*
"ELDERLY MARBLE
MOUTH"

The NPR control center

Amy Dickinson

We received the prestigious Peabody Award for Morning Edition *and* Wait Wait.

When I think back about my newscasting career at NPR, I recall looking out the window as the sun was rising. Washington was like a sleeping giant, just stretching and waking up, and getting ready to go about its business. To know that I was helping start the day for the capital of the most powerful nation in the world ... I feel good about that. — Carl Kasell plains how the decision was made to give my voice on their answering machine as a prize.

I can't say for absolute certain, but I recall that the idea first came from one of our early producers, Leslie Fuller. We had no prize, because there was no money for a prize. And to me, having a "real" prize felt tacky. I didn't think people were tuning in to our show to win a prize. So when Leslie suggested that jokingly, we embraced it. It was a prize that was both priceless and worthless, perfect for Wait Wait.

They asked if I would do the home answering machine messages — this was before digital voice mail had become widely used — for a short time until we had a budget and we could buy some gifts. Well, "a short time" never ended. I've been doing them ever since, and as of this writing, have recorded over 3,000 messages. The winning listener gets to write what I say or sing. Many are pretty straight, but I have recorded a message as if I was a family's cat and sung verses of everything from Broadway musicals, to Aerosmith songs, to rap. Below are some of my favorite messages:

This is Carl Kasell of National Public Radio news. Reliable sources report that both Mike and Carla are not available to answer the phone right now. We have verified that they do not need siding, windows or a hot tub, and their carpets are clean. They give to charity through the office, and they don't need their picture taken. If you're still with me, leave your name and number, and they'll get back to you soon. And thanks.

Hello, you've reached the voice mail of Amy, Michael and Helen. And, yes, all you NPR listeners, this is Carl Kasell. Now surely, you're not calling just to hear the dulcet tones of my voice, but if you are? Get a life. Otherwise, leave a message for the Salvadores. Wait Wait, don't tell me until you hear the beep.

(Carl speaks as if to himself) You know, imagine a professional of my caliber making messages as a game show prize ... You don't see Bob Edwards giving his voice away, or Terry Gross or Daniel Schorr being asked to stoop so low. I feel so ... cheap! Oh well, I guess it's not such a bad gig, all things considered.

Oh, you still here? Have a nice day.

178

Hello, I'm Carl Kasell from NPR. Jennifer and I have eloped. Please leave your message at the beep.

Hello, this is Carl Kasell of National Public Radio. David hopes that your message can keep, because he's out, tied up, or asleep. But don't panic, don't swoon, he'll get back to you soon, if you'll just leave your name at the _____.

From this message, it's perfectly clear,
That we've risen in status this year.
Carl Kasell's the voice,
And you've got just one choice:
Leave a message 'cause no one is _____.

Hello, this is Carl Kasell from National Public Radio. Kristin and George are not available at this time. But before you leave a message, I'd like to sing you a little tune.
(Carl singing) What's new, pussycat? Whoa, whoa, whoa, whoa. What's new, pussycat? Whoa, whoa, whoa, whoa, whoa.

(Carl singing) OOOOOOklahoma, where the wind comes sweeping down the plain. (Carl speaking) Howdy! This is Carl Kasell of National Public Radio. Renee and Brian can't come to the phone, so please leave a message. And remember, the farmer and the cow man should be friends. Yahoooooooo!

(Carl in an echo chamber) Hello, this is Carl Kasell of National Public Radio. Jane and Christy have imprisoned me

in a rabbit hutch in their basement. Please! In the name of all that is dear to you, send help! I am — (interrupted by child's voice)
Mom, Carl's doing it again!
(Carl's voice, softer but urgent) Sorry, I have to go. Leave a message.

Hello, this is Carl Kasell of National Public Radio. After Steve won the Listener Limerick Challenge, he pleaded with the producers of this show to have Click and Clack from Car Talk *record the message on his home answering machine. This is MY GIG! Can you believe that schmuck? Jody and Steve have some nerve. If you still want to talk with them, I GUESS you can leave a message. I wouldn't, if I were you.*

My son, Joe, when he heard about the prize, said, "Who would want your voice on their answering machine?" Apparently not everyone. When you call our home phone, the voice on the message is Mary Ann's.

I thoroughly enjoy Peter, the staff and all of the panelists, and we really are like one big, happy family. In 2002, Adam Felber was getting married. He sent me an e-mail: "Carl, would you preside at my wedding? Don't worry, it'll be legal. We're getting married at City Hall in the morning. We'd like you to preside at the wedding that night."

I replied, "Will you write the script?"

He said he would.

"I'll do it," I said. So I flew to New York, and as we were standing in front of the couple's family and friends, the best man pretended that he couldn't find the wedding rings. As he fumbled around in panic, I told the gathering, "Don't worry." I raised my arms. "It's floating around here in the air." Using one of my magic tricks, I grabbed something out of the air and clenched it in my fist. Slowly, I pulled a small silk handkerchief out of my fist, opened it, and inside were, of course, the rings. As you can imagine with a man like Adam, it was a perfect way to start what would be a very funny wedding, one joke after another.

Shortly before I remarried in 2003, Mary Ann asked, "Do you think Peter would preside at our wedding?"

I said, "I don't know. Call him up and ask." She did, and he jumped at it. Peter flew in, and the whole crew from *Wait Wait* came down from New York and from other places far and wide for the wedding. Bob Edwards did a reading, as did Jean Cochran and Adam Felber. Adam inserted ad-libs into his reading, and it was very funny. Peter, of course, set the tone. Mary Ann and I had been an item for a while. Peter opened the ceremony by saying, "Welcome," and blah, blah, blah, blah. "This just in: Carl Kasell and Mary Ann Foster are no longer living in sin!"

Oh, Peter.

Phil Hauck

Carl was the anchor of the show. He was the ballast. The whole reason Wait Wait *works is because listeners know the humor is grounded in actual news. Carl's voice and presence conveyed that.*

Because Carl's presence anchored us to reality, the rest of the cast was free to make stuff up, and make us laugh. That tension ... that true grounding in reality paired with the humor ... is what makes Wait Wait *different from every other comedy show on radio or TV. And it's really thanks to Carl, the glue that created the center and held it together.*

— Doug Berman, Wait Wait...Don't Tell Me! *creator*

paula poundstone

I am happy to take a moment to write a few words about Carl Kasell, and I hope he gets into this college.

Like many, I had listened to Carl broadcast the morning news for lots of years before I discovered him on *Wait Wait...Don't Tell Me!* There, on that quirky little news quiz show, I found the voice that I had come to trust for intelligent information doing falsetto Britney Spears imitations. Carl is game. He dove right into the silly, usually with a straight face, or just the merest chuckle.

Wait Wait...Don't Tell Me! had been on the air for a couple of years when I showed up, but we were still doing the shows via wire, each of us in a different location, with no live audience. So I didn't see Carl in the flesh until I had been on for at least a few months. I don't remember the first occasion of meeting him.

I can tell you that I was in the midst of hellacious personal problems around the time we first met, and he always greeted me with a welcoming hug and asked after my family, which I deeply appreciated.

He is tremendously proud of his own son and grandchildren, and often tells me about them.

From the moment I first saw him on the *Wait Wait* stage the audience loved him. He would run across the stage when introduced and high five each of the panelists, as if we were on a gym floor in the midst of March Madness. Honestly, I never know if he knew it was funny, or if he had just always wanted to do that. Whatever, the crowd ate it up.

When we are done with the show, the director and producers will often have a few lines that they need one or the other of us to repeat for various reasons. They tell each of us in our headphones, so no one else hears what we're about to do. There was something so damned funny about listening to Carl say, "Okay, now?" and then repeat a line like an angry politician or Snooki. The more ridiculous, the more seriously he went about trying to get it right. If I had to guess, I'd say he wouldn't know Snooki if he tripped over her.

I have heard that they originally came up with the prize of "Carl Kasell's voice on your answering machine" because they had no money for prizes, and it was kind of a stop-gap measure until they could afford to offer something else. The prize, however, became so popular, they never replaced it. People are forever asking me if I have Carl's voice on my answering machine and inquiring as to how they might get it. I do not, by the way, because I don't win very often.

After we finished the retakes, Peter usually asked the crowd if they had any questions for us, and often someone would ask how Carl does the answering machine messages. After he told them that he flew around in the NPR jet, he would confess that people sent in a CD plus a script, and he would go into the studio every so often and record a bunch. He would then ask if they wanted to hear one, and they always did. So the engineer would fire up one of Carl's recorded answering machine messages. Again, the funniest part was how professionally he attended to whatever the winner asked him to do, whether it was pretending to cry for help while trapped in a rabbit cage, or belting out a chorus of *What's New Pussycat?*

I'm glad he's still doing the answering machine messages,

even though he has retired as the show's announcer/scorekeeper. I don't think people want anyone else's voice on their answering machine. Carl is beloved.

Twenty-five years ago, Paula Poundstone climbed on a Greyhound bus and traveled across the country, stopping in at open mic nights at comedy clubs as she went. A high school dropout, she went on to become one of the great humorists of our time. You can hear her through your laughter as a regular panelist on NPR's popular rascal of a weekly news quiz show, Wait Wait...Don't Tell Me! *Paula tours regularly, performing her stand-up comedy across the country, causing Bob Zany with the* Boston Globe *to write: "Poundstone can regale an audience for several hours with her distinctive brand of wry, intelligent and witty comedy." Audience members may put it a little less elegantly: "I peed my pants." www. paulapoundstone.com*

In Colorado Springs, Colorado, during a 2010 pre-show audience warmup before a sold out crowd of 2,000, Peter Sagal had some fun with Carl's popularity.

Peter: *Honestly, it's amazing. I love this. One of my favorite things when we do a show like this, is when we open the show and it sounds like: "Paul Provenza, yay;" "Tom Bodett, yay;" "Faith Salie, yay;" "Carl Kasell, YAYYYYYYY!"*

(loud laughter)

Carl: *Some of us have it, Peter.*

(loud laughter)

Peter: *It's like this is a mega-church in here and Jesus just walked in.*

(loud laughter)

mo rocca

Here's something completely unsurprising: I liked Carl the minute I met him, and I wanted him to like me. A broadcasting legend with a lifetime of stories (Andy Griffith was his drama teacher!), Carl is warm and cool. I used to tell people, "Even if you loved both your grandfathers, you'd trade one in for Carl" ... until I realized that wasn't accurate at all. He's not old enough to be my grandpa. In fact, the man embodies young at heart.

I remember sitting in an airport lounge with him 10 or 11 years ago. I can't remember where we were. It was the morning after a taping. I was headed home. Carl was heading solo to Italy. He said his late wife was Italian and he was going to visit her family. I thought, "Jeez, don't most widows and widowers drape themselves in black until they maybe meet someone else? Don't they lose contact with the departed spouse's family? Wouldn't hanging out with them be a constant downer, like reliving the funeral over and over again?"

But there was nothing lugubrious about Carl at all. He was excited to see them. I wish I could remember exactly what he said but it was something to the effect of, "I loved her and I love her family, so, of course, I want to see them. And who doesn't love Italy?" I realized this is a man who loves to live, who's always moving forward. And so it made perfect sense when he started dating, then married, Mary Ann, another lover of life, a woman lit from within. There was nothing "second marriage" about their wedding. They may as well have been 25-year-olds tying the knot for the first time.

One day, Roy Blount, Jr. and I were trading travel-to-Chicago-in-the-winter horror stories. (Roy's a got a great one about a passenger whose butt ended up in his face.) We both realized that Carl — who did the show every week, not just occasionally like the panelists — had only once missed one show due to flight cancellation. Like us, he was flying from the East Coast, but he almost never had weather delays. There's no escaping it: wherever Carl is, it's sunny.

Mo Rocca

With young-at-heart Carl, backstage at a Wait Wait *taping*

Humorist, journalist and actor Mo Rocca is best known for his off-beat news reports and satirical commentary. In addition to appearing on Wait Wait, he's a correspondent for CBS Sunday Morning, *and is the host and creator of the Cooking Channel's* My Grandmother's Ravioli, *in which he learns to cook from grandmothers and grandfathers across the country. Rocca served as a correspondent on Comedy Central's* The Daily Show with Jon Stewart, *and on* The Tonight Show with Jay Leno.

roxanne roberts

You know what would be a bust? A Carl Kasell roast. The problem, as Peter puts it, is that are aren't many great Carl stories because really great stories need a punch line. And Carl, bless his sweet North Carolinian soul, has never done anything that merits a punch line.

You can trust me on this: As an original panelist on *Wait Wait,* I spent 16 years in tiny radio studios, taxicabs, green rooms and other off-stage settings and never saw an unkind moment, a snide aside, a dark cloud pass over his face. I never heard him say a mean thing about anyone, ever, even people who totally deserved it. Carl was so relentlessly good — without being a goodie-goodie — that he forced me to be a better person and try very, very hard not to curse in front of him.

Clearly, a hopeless subject for a roast or any other mockery.

For the first few years, *Wait Wait* was recorded from separate cities — wherever the host and panelists happened to be that week — and Carl and I sat across from each other in studios at NPR headquarters in Washington. I'd rush in at the last minute, slap on the earphones, and we'd tape the show. I became his back-up scorekeeper, carefully marking down points as if it mattered. (It did, to me, because I took ridiculous delight in winning. Still do. Sue me.) We bonded over silly jokes and bad puns and all those technical glitches that kept popping up. Sometimes, I brought homemade cookies because if anyone deserved cookies, it was Carl.

When the show began taping in front of live audiences in Chicago, he became a frequent flyer god and racked up all those points that made him a platinum-titanium-diamond traveler that the airlines fawn over. We usually took the same flight back to DC after a show, which meant we shared a pre-dawn cab to the airport and breakfast in those fancy VIP lounges before the flights. When we landed, I always got a hug and always walked away with a smile.

Everybody else can tell how great Carl was on the show. I can tell you how great he was when no one else was listening. There were hundreds of small moments — before I had coffee, mind you — when we talked about kids and grandkids and pets. We pulled out our phones and proudly shared photos of babies and puppies and cats because it made us both happy. Everyone says Carl is a gentleman, but Faith calls him a "gentle man" and that's exactly right: A man who appreciates the fleeting, often overlooked, pleasures of life with no bluster or apologies.

Carl's last *Wait Wait* show was taped in Washington with tributes from Stephen Colbert, Tom Hanks, Katie Couric and President Obama, which caused him and the 1,800 people packed into the Warner Theatre to all get a little choked up. The crowd, as they say, went wild. We are talking public radio fans, so that meant standing ovations and extended applause, not underwear tossed on stage. At the end of the taping, they politely mobbed Carl like he was Springsteen or the Pope.

Which, in a weird way, he is — The Boss of Good.

Roxanne Roberts has been a reporter at The Washington Post *for 26 years covering Washington's A-listers, powerbrokers and other saints and scoundrels. She has one son, two Siamese cats and about 500 cookie cutters.*

I will never forget the day that Carl Kasell married me.

It was a snowy December afternoon in Manhattan, and even though it was 2002 and it wasn't strictly legal in New York, that wonderful man went ahead and married me, and yes, I was his first. But it's not what you think. Unless what you think is, "Oh, I see: Carl officiated at the wedding of you and your wife, even though he wasn't ordained to do so in the state of New York." In which case, yes, it is, in fact, exactly what you think.

And so, at dawn on our wedding day, Jeanne and I headed down to City Hall to get the "official" version of something that wouldn't be real to us until it was sanctified by *Wait Wait*'s official judge and scorekeeper. We'd known Carl for several years at that point, and neither of us could think of anyone on the planet who was capable of conveying the same gravitas, good humor, warmth, and gentle, but unquestionable, authority as Carl Kasell.

I remember him being a bit surprised when I asked him, though he agreed readily. Me, I was shocked to learn that this was his first gig as a hitcher. The idea seemed so obvious and right to us that we thought hundreds of couples would've already called upon his services. Had he wanted to, Carl could've filled vast stadiums with betrothed NPR-loving couples, giving the followers of Reverend Sung Myung Moon fits of envy. [After all, when the Unification Church marries you, you never get a tote bag.]

But no, Carl chose a different path. I remember on the weekend of the wedding talking to his girlfriend, the amazing Mary Ann Foster. She confided that Carl was feeling more nervous about the ceremony than he had before just about any previous performance. Which was touching, but he needn't have worried. Come on. He's Carl Kasell.

I don't remember all of the lines I wrote for him. I do remember this, though. When it was just about over, he concluded the proceedings with this line:

"And now, by the power vested in me by my extremely recognizable and trustworthy voice, I pronounce you husband and wife."

How awesome is that?

Jeanne and I kissed and then led the recessional as our chosen music played. It was Boots Randolph's "Yakety Sax," by the way, the beloved ditty from the end of the *The Benny Hill Show.* You know, because a recessional looks a little like a low-speed chase. I bring this up not because Carl was especially involved in this, but because I think it was a pretty cool move, even if a couple of the bridesmaids seemed not to think so.

But it was a great day. Lots of *Wait Wait*'s early stalwarts were there, including Roxanne Roberts and Charlie Pierce. Mo Rocca was one of my groomsmen, and Roy Blount, Jr. had offered a great toast at the rehearsal dinner the night before. I don't remember everything he said, but it involved beets and it made my mom chuckle wickedly.

Two of Peter Sagal's three lovely daughters served as our flower girls. The third, Willa, declined to participate on the grounds that she was still, in fact, in utero, but to be honest, I still take that as a bit of a slight.

One last detail — the ceremony was literally magical. A little-known but true fact is that Carl is an avid amateur magician, a skill that one rarely gets to show off on the radio. So in order to bring his gifts to a wider audience, I built a trick into the ceremony. When the time came, my best man (and sketch comedy partner) Michael Bernard turned out to have misplaced the ring! All was lost. Until, with a flourish, Carl produced the missing item, wrapped in a red silk handkerchief, out of thin air!*

Not long afterwards, Carl came to me with a special request: Would I consider doing a reading at his upcoming nuptials with the lovely Mary Ann? My first thought was "Copycat!" But my second was, of course, "Of course!" Their vows were solemnified in a ceremony in Georgetown, presided over by the Right Reverend Peter Sagal, the world's only fiery Baptist preacher who is, in point of fact, a Jew.

Almost exactly eight years later, Carl Kasell returned to Manhattan, this time to do *Wait Wait...Don't Tell Me!* at a sold-out Carnegie Hall, right down the street from where my wedding had been. It was a great night, and it made me remember how eight years earlier, Jeanne and I had been told that the reason Carl couldn't administer our actual, legal vows was because he was not a pastor who maintained an active congregation in the state of New York. Looking out at the 3,000 adoring fans inside that fantastic, glittering temple to the arts, hanging on Carl's every word, I had to think that City Hall had totally blown that call.

---

*Sorry, Carl, but it's been 12 years. I'm telling how you did it! It was a ████ █████ ████. (*Redacted by author. It was magic, Adam.*)

Adam Felber is a sketch comedy performer, actor and writer for Real Time with Bill Maher. *He is the author of the 2006 novel* Schrodinger's Ball. *Adam's work can be seen and heard all around TV and the Internet, as well as on the pages of Marvel Comics' recent* Skrull Kill Krew *miniseries. Other writing credits include* Lewis Black's Root of All Evil, Talkshow with Spike Feresten *and* Wishbone.

Carl is so low-key, I can't think of what you might call "Carl stories." (Well, aside from his announcing at his retirement party that he didn't want anybody to get the notion that he was retiring.) But he has certainly been a great figure in the story of *Wait Wait*.

Doug Berman told me once that his concept of the show began with Carl — in the role played by George Fenneman in Groucho Marx's quiz show, *You Bet Your Life*. I would say that Peter and the rest of us, altogether, are better than Groucho; but Carl, alone, is much better than Fenneman. Fenneman was a dweeby straight man, readily flustered. Carl has always been august and unflappable.

In connection with Groucho, the temptation arises to compare Carl with Margaret Dumont. But there's never been any doubt that Carl was in on the joke. And consider his voices. Ms. Dumont had only the one, which Carl could have done (may have done, for all I know) a memorable version of. Carl's voices, from Peggy Lee to Vladimir Putin, have been all the more marvelously dubious for issuing from such an unimpeachable source. In the midst of panelists' hoots and babble, Carl's gravitas would surface as a constant element of surprise.

In the dreary early episodes, before Peter became the host, Carl was the only part that clicked. And he kept up the beat as the band came together around him.

Joan Griswold/www.royblountjr.com

One of the first panelists on Wait Wait...Don't Tell Me!, *and an original member of the Rock Bottom Remainders, Roy Blount, Jr. is the author of 23 books, about everything from the first woman president of the United States to what barnyard animals are thinking. He is ex-president of the Authors Guild, a member of PEN and the Fellowship of Southern Authors, a New York Public Library Literary Lion, a Boston Public Library Literary Light, and a usage consultant to the American Heritage Dictionary. He grew up in Decatur, Georgia, and lives in Western Massachusetts and New Orleans.*

When Carl's NPR friends threw a going-away party for him in 2014, everyone was getting up to say a few things about him and toast his wonderfulness. And I noticed that there was a sameness to the salutes, about how sweet, kind and decent he was. That's what happens when you lead a life of such consistency. It's like talking about someone on Mount Rushmore.

The monotony of acclaim had to stop. So when it was my turn, I stood up and said, "I hate to be the one to tell the crowd, but I once saw Carl shoot a man in Reno just to watch him die." I continued, "And you've all neglected to mention that animal magnetism! How Carl drives the women wild. We can't resist him!" He was seated across the room from me, and as he sat there smiling, I pointed. "There it is! That animal magnetism. He's doing it again. Stop it, Carl!"

I've known Carl for a very long time. The thing about Carl is that he's such a gentleman and he's so lovely. And he is one of those people, no matter how busy, who always act the same, never flustered, and he's always seemed to pace himself so beautifully. Maybe that's how you get to be so high-functioning at 80. In the earlier days at NPR, when deadlines approached, people got tense and voices got loud; cursing wasn't unusual. But Carl always kept his cool. And that's part of his appeal. I'm not sure how he does that.

At the time I met him while working at NPR in Washington,

I was a single mother with a young daughter, Emily, who had no grandparents around. I would sometimes bring her to work with me, and she got to know Carl. He was the only person she had spent time with who had a grandfatherly presence and, of course, Carl was very approachable. Emily is so, so fond of him.

Amy Dickinson

With my good friend, Carl, at a Wait, Wait *taping*

When Emily was five years old, I took her to the NPR Christmas party. Carl and Barry Gordemer entertained the group with their magic act, something Carl often did on his own, too. And he was so good at it. As Carl and Barry sawed Nina Totenberg in half, Emily nervously asked, "What is happening, Mommy?"

After Carl's wife, Clara, died, he seemed lost. He'd always had a punishing schedule and obviously had been treated really well by Clara, but he was sad and grieving. I was glad to see Carl come back to life when he and Mary Ann started dating. My daughter and I, just by sheer coincidence, ran into them on their first date. Mary Ann is wonderful, and I feel fortunate to have gotten to know her. She's been a wonderful companion and an advocate for Carl. A true mate.

I have the distinct honor of being an original cast member of *Wait Wait...Don't Tell Me!* At the pilot taping, I was sitting next to Carl at a table with microphones, and it struck me what brilliant casting, inspired casting, it was when they hired Carl. You're taking this incredibly avuncular newsman and putting him in a very funny position. And yet, it is a position of leadership because he is the official scorekeeper and judge.

When you see this man with a lovely presence come out on the stage at the *Wait Wait* tapings, people start to scream. He drives the women crazy! Does he get that these women are screaming for him? It's so NPR funny. They did a great job of playing off of that, like creating the Carl Kasell pillow. People love him, revere him and want to meet him. He's consistently lovely and so courtly and affectionate, and he brings out the best in people. He's such a good performer. I've known Carl for 20 years and I'm still not sure he's in on the joke, which is the brilliance of his straight man persona.

Amy Dickinson is a syndicated advice columnist, penning the "Ask Amy" column, which appears in more than 100 newspapers. Her background as a dairy farmer's daughter and lounge singer prepared her to be a panelist on NPR's Wait Wait...Don't Tell Me! *Her commentaries and radio stories also have been featured on* All Things Considered.

memories from
brian babylon

One day about four years before I started on *Wait Wait*, I was working on another radio station in the WBEZ building in Chicago, Vocalo, and saw Carl walking down the hallway. "Oh s---, that's Carl Kasell!" And I ran to get my camera. We took a picture together (shown below) and I posted it on Facebook. All my friends went crazy. "Oh man, you met Carl Kasell? Wow!" I was so excited to meet him.

I'm one of the newer panelists, but I've been aware of the popularity of *Wait Wait* for a long time. And the heartbeat of the show is Carl. I'm amazed at his showmanship, comedic timing and professionalism. My favorite "Carl voice" is the lady voice. Carl Kasell's lady voice is so funny, kind of like Dolly Parton with a chest cold. It's genius.

Carl's always been so nice to me. We have North Carolina in common because, of course, he's from there and my mom moved there about ten years ago. My sister went to Duke, which has a historic rivalry with the Tar Heels in basketball. And, oh, we love to talk basketball! Carl lit up when he found out that I went to basketball camp with former UNC stars Jerry Stackhouse and Eric Montross. Carl and I talk hoops, hang out and chill. Good times.

To be associated with his legacy is such an honor, and I have Chicago's bad weather to thank for it. *Wait Wait* executive producer Mike Danforth and senior producer Ian Chillag were aware of my stand-up comedy act and came to a couple of my shows. On occasion, some panelists were snowed out of Chicago, so I was invited on to fill in, and I hit the ground running and never looked back.

Here's how cool Carl is. Say you're on an airplane and you're having the worst day ever. You don't want anything to do with the stranger in the next seat, let alone talk to him. But, if it's Carl? You'd forget you were having a bad day. He's so genuine, such a unique individual, cut from a cloth that is no longer made. And his wife, Mary Ann, is the sweetest thing and makes me feel so good. She thinks I'm funny. Mary Ann and Carl are my heart.

Here's my idea, and I think it's a big one: Now that Carl's retired, he and Mary Ann can adopt me, an old black comic, and we can call the show *The Blind Side II*. It would be the zany adventures of Carl, Mary Ann and me. It would be hot!

Brian Babylon

Brian Babylon is a Chicago-born comic and radio host. The self-proclaimed "Prince of Bronzeville," he is a fixture in Chicago's rich comedy community. He's also been making a name for himself outside of Chicago, placing in the finals of the New York Comedy Contest in 2009. He has performed in L.A. at the historic Laugh Factory, and in the U.K. at Jongleurs comedy club in London. Currently, Brian hosts and produces The Morning AMp *radio show on Vocalo 89.5FM, a sister station of Chicago Public Radio. Along with* Wait Wait...Don't Tell Me, *Brian contributes to BBC Radio and hosts* The Moth Story SLAM *in Chicago. Twitter: @brianbabylon.*

Nobody prepared me for what happened when I first appeared on *Wait Wait* as a panelist in 2009. Before the show began, the panelists were introduced, and we all stood behind our table to a nice round of applause, and then Carl was introduced. I was not expecting to see this 75-year-old man run out from the wings, like *run* out onto the stage and high-five each of us on the way to his podium as the crowd went absolutely wild!

For me, a *Wait Wait* fan long before I joined the show, it was just thrilling to meet the man himself. And the bonus was to find out very quickly how lovable, warm and human he is.

I honestly don't know, even after six years on the show with Carl, whether he is a comic genius on purpose or by accident. I don't know if he sat there beforehand thinking that this would be a funny way to say it, or if stuff just comes out of his mouth and it's funny just because Carl Kasell said it. And I don't ever want to know.

On the one hand, Carl has this magnificent deadpan delivery and the voice of authority that also has some folksiness in it, but on the other hand, he can really gin up the funny and the enthusiasm. He's asked to do so many accents and ladies' voices, and part of the hilarity is that no matter what voice he's asked to do, he doesn't do it very well, because it always sounds like Carl — and I say that as a compliment. It's like when Johnny Carson used to do Carnac the Magnificent, or Art Fern or other characters, it was still always Johnny Carson; he could never do impersonations very well, but it was hilarious.

I was nervous when I started on the show because being on *Wait Wait...Don't Tell Me!*, to me, is like being a member of The Beatles. People love that show so much. So I wanted to rise to the quality of the other panelists and be funny, and be smart, and I was really nervous about it. Carl made me feel welcome and comfortable from day one, and every time I'd come back, he would immediately have the warmest smile and hug.

Early on in my time at *Wait Wait*, the cast and crew would usually go out after shows for a drink. Often times, Carl and I were the first to leave the scene, and we'd share a taxi back to the hotel. This is when we were staying at the Chicago Club, not far from the Chase Bank Auditorium in Chicago's Loop. I had recently been divorced and was dating, and as we were riding up the elevator, for some reason I felt comfortable talking to a man in his seventies about my love life and my quest for love again. And Carl was — it was so touching — Carl was so forthcoming about how he had lost his first wife and she was a true love of his, and how he had met Mary Ann, and how she is another true love of his and how lucky he felt. He told me that life can throw you curveballs, but that love can come again when you least expect it. He made me feel incredibly hopeful.

And it was so funny because he was giving me this pep talk on the elevator, and we had reached his floor and the doors opened, but we were still talking. I didn't want him to get off the elevator, so I kept hitting the "Door Open" button because I didn't want him to stop his story. We were holding up the elevator for the whole place, so finally, I gave him a hug good night and thanked him. It was so kind and generous of Carl to offer that much of himself and be that self-revelatory and encouraging to me.

A very short time later, I met the man who would become my second husband and Carl was delighted for me, and even more so when he heard that John and I were going to get married in Rome. Carl told me about his time in Verona when he was stationed there and how he met his first wife there. And now that John and I have kids, it never fails, Carl always asks me about them, how they're doing.

Carl is the consummate gentleman. I never saw him with a hair out of place, he's always dressed to the nines in a suit, and always had the most gallant hug and kiss on the cheek.

One of the *Wait Wait* gifts is the Carl Kasell Pillow, and I just have to think that it gives so many ladies the sweetest dreams!

Faith Salie is an American actress, comedian, radio host, and television personality, and is probably the only Rhodes scholar who's been a standup comedian. www.faithsalie.com

After a *Wait Wait* taping in Chicago, Carl and I shared a cab to O'Hare and while making our way through the terminal, we came to some big escalators. I jumped on the magic stairs, while Carl — over 20 years my senior — bounded up the regular stairs beside me.

"Look at you, Carl!" says I.

He was unimpressed with himself and simply told me, "If you want to keep doing it, you better keep doing it."

I've taken the stairs ever since.

bodett.com

Humorist, radio personality, voice actor, and author, Tom Bodett joined Wait Wait *as a regular panelist in 2005. He is the only cast member to have appeared as a* Not My Job *guest, substituted for Carl Kasell, worked as a panelist, AND guest-hosted for Peter Sagal. This distinction, Tom points out, means nothing.*

"**M**argaret, doing *Wait Wait...Don't Tell Me!* is like crack cocaine!" We were sitting in the theater before a *Wait Wait* show in Boulder, Colorado when I first took over the program. Carl was describing the profound pleasure he got from doing *Wait Wait*. Carl loved the job and the audience loved him back. We always joked that, after the show, the lines of people for Doug Berman, the executive producer, were long; the lines for host Peter Sagal were longer; and the lines for Carl were the longest. He had a way of touching people and everyone wanted a chance to meet him.

I came to NPR's *Morning Edition* in February of 1982 as an overnight production assistant. He was the newscaster and was the most senior and authoritative presence there. We used to joke that we could set our watch to when Carl got to work. He would arrive right on the nose at 2 a.m. It was so reassuring to see Carl walk through the door. In those early days, he looked like he had just stepped out of the 1950s, wearing black, horn-rimmed glasses, a butch haircut and a short-sleeved, button-down shirt. He was always so calm, cool and in charge. And yet, he had this sweet, funny and charming side to him that the public only got to see when he started doing *Wait Wait*.

I took over *Wait Wait* in the early 2000s, and Carl was part of that team. So I was his boss, too. For about 10 years, he was doing both the newscasts and *Wait Wait*. I took him out to lunch one day and asked if he would like to do just *Wait Wait*. And he was thrilled.

He was having so much fun doing the show, but worried that if he gave up newscasting after 30 years, he would also lose *Wait Wait*.

Carl was the perfect person for the job because he was Peter's straight man, but what we all knew about Carl, and others were beginning to learn, was that he loved performing. He had a background in theater and performance, and there was always a sense of play in Carl even though he was a serious newsman.

Even though Carl stepped away from doing the weekly show, nearly everyday he still comes to NPR where he has an "office for life." He loved to visit my office, and left with fistfuls of chocolate candy.

Carl loves NPR and he cherishes the work he still does for NPR, including the voicemail messages for *Wait Wait*. He's a connector and cares about his relationships with people. Carl is kind, good and just a decent human being.

Margaret Low Smith is the President of AtlanticLIVE. She was most recently NPR Senior Vice President for News. In that role, she oversaw NPR's News Division and the work of nearly 400 broadcast and digital journalists across the country and in 17 bureaus around the world.

I grab something invisible to
the audience that I see floating
through the air ...

... clutch it in my
fist and slowly
open it up ...

... and reveal a bright
red handkerchief!

magic edition

"From NPR News in Washington, I'm Carl Kasell." That's often the first thing I say when I take the stage at public appearances. It creates an instant connection with audiences who have heard my voice but may not have seen my face. There's an instant recognition: "Oh, that's Carl."

Another great icebreaker is magic. One of my favorite tricks begins with me giving an envelope to an audience member. I tell them I wrote it last night before I went to bed, put it in the envelope and sealed it. I say, "Do not open it until I tell you to."

Then I hold up a page out of a newspaper that has a column cut out of it and tell the audience that I saw a story that morning I was interested in and clipped it out. I hold up the clipping and a pair of scissors, and I ask another audience member to tell me where to cut the column. I tell them they can change their mind if they want. No guiding from me. I cut the paper, it falls to the floor, and I back away. The audience member picks it up.

I say, "You told me where to cut the paper, right?"

They agree.

"Okay, hold on to that for a moment."

Then I turn to the audience member holding the envelope and tell them to open it.

"Read what I wrote the night before."

They do.

Alaska Public Radio

I turn back to the person holding the clipping.

"What is the first line of the paper?"

They read the first line aloud. It is not the same as what was in the envelope.

I don't say anything for a moment, giving the audience the impression that my trick went bad. "There must be something wrong," I say. "Turn it over."

They do, and they read the first line under the cut aloud, and it's the exact same thing as was in the envelope. It always gets a great response. Magic has been so much fun for me, and audiences seem to really enjoy it. That newspaper trick is actually one that's ridiculously easy to do, but it's a real head-scratcher for people. It's a wonderful feeling, and I also like doing that one because it has a connection to the news.

Barry Gordemer, a longtime producer and director at NPR, taught me so much about magic. He's an amazing magician, a great friend, and I've asked him to say a few words:

I joined Morning Edition as a director in 1987 and also worked as a professional magician. I was known in the Washington area as "The Sort of Amazing Barry." A lot of times, if I was working on a new trick, I would try it out on my colleagues at work. They were very patient with me. I showed some of the tricks to Carl and he would really get into them. So for Christmas one year, around 1992 or 1993, I got him a magic trick. It was a deck of cards where some-body would pick a card and put it back in the deck. Then the card would float; it would rise up out of the deck. Carl loved it and was showing it to everybody, and over time, I showed him more things and bought him other tricks as gifts. Eventually, we worked up a little magic act, which we called, "Magic Edition." We would perform at NPR parties and events, including public radio conferences where news directors and station managers from member stations across the country would meet in a city somewhere and talk about all things public radio.

There used to be an annual magician's convention in Washington, DC. One of the companies that sold tricks and props at the event was Stevens Magic Emporium based in Wichita, Kansas. It was run by Joe Stevens and his daughter, Amy, who was a writer and graphic designer. Another magi-cian knew that she was a big NPR fan and he told me, "Oh, you've got to meet Amy." Stevens sells magic tricks all over the world and became famous for instructional videos where some of the world's best magicians would perform, and then show you how to do the tricks. Those video tapes were host-ed by Amy, who eventually became my wife. I shared some of those tapes with Carl, and so he sort of got to know Amy through the videos, and when she would come to Washington as we were doing our long distance dating, Carl would want to greet her and talk about magic. We all built quite a good relationship.

Stevens Magic Emporium used to host a big convention in Las Vegas where about a thousand magicians from all over the world would gather to perform, teach each other magic tricks and sell stuff. Amy helped run that convention and one year, 1996 or '97, she invited Carl and me to the convention. It was great! We saw Siegfried and Roy, which was such an over-the-top Las Vegas show with the show-girls, laser lights and a fire-breathing dragon. I remember Carl just laughing in the middle of all of it, turning to me and saying, "Ain't THAT something!"

I taught Carl how to make doves appear out of nowhere and disappear. Carl always liked something that had a news theme in the magic act. One time, he presented the results of the latest NPR News Poll, and he reached into a small sand-wich bag and started to pull out a pole, and continued to pull, and pull, and pull. The pole was basically a telescoping wooden stick that was eight feet tall. That was Carl and the NPR News Poll.

One of the things that makes Carl so beloved by audiences is the instant connection he creates. He has that natural sense of theater about him, and a natural ability to connect with an audience. For many broadcasters, sitting behind a microphone in a soundproof studio, the audience is an ab-stract concept. For Carl, it's a very real thing. He under-stands that connection. Carl never fit the image, for me, of what a big time newscaster should be. He was always so approachable and friendly and good natured. There was not this hard, gruff, rumpled sort of stereotype you think of: the old journalist with a nose for news and a nose for booze. Carl was always upbeat and pleasant. He always seemed to be enjoying what he was doing.

At the NPR Christmas party one year, Carl and I had re-hearsed our magic act and we were going to saw somebody in half. We didn't know who. As we were unloading our stuff, we ran into Nina Totenberg in the parking garage. We said, "Nina, would you be willing to be our volunteer?" We didn't tell her for what.

She said, "Oh yes, I'd love to." Nina, like Carl, is 100 percent ham through and through. So we got her up on stage, and Carl and I put together a routine. Imagine that magnifi-cent voice coupled with an Orson Welles sense of drama as he was wielding an electric saw and cutting people in half. He would be completely straight and completely hamming it up at the same time, and everybody got it, everybody got the joke. I'll throw it back to Carl for the rest of that story.

Nina was a great sport. We had her recline on a table and then placed a wooden stock, a wooden form that looked like a miniature bridge, over her waist. Then we turned on the Black and Decker electric saw, made a lot of noise with it, and used it to cut a piece of French bread in half to show it was a real saw. Then, Barry and I turned to the audience.

"This was really messy last time," I told him and the audi-ence. "I hope we do a better job this time."

We placed the saw on the edge of the wooden frame, and before we turned it on, we touched the saw to Nina's belly.

218

"Can you feel that?" I asked.

"Yes, I can!" she screamed.

So Barry and I put down the saw and whipped out our giant-sized magician's instruction book to see where we'd gone wrong. After a few seconds of poring over it and murmuring between the two of us, we put the book away, looked at the audience and said, "Never mind, never mind," and proceeded to saw her in half. Then we took out a roll of duct tape and taped her back together and she was none the worse for wear. Nina said it tickled.

After most of my tricks, people ask, "How did you do that?"

I always say, "I think very well!"

Barry Gordemer

Barry Gordemer, my magic mentor, and I astound a 1994 NPR Christmas party with a giant card trick.

— eleven —

the kennedy center honors

One day in 2007, I received a telephone call at NPR from a man named Michael Stevens. He told me that he woke up every weekday morning listening to me, was very complimentary of my work on the radio and told me that my style would be perfect as the announcer for the *Kennedy Center Honors* show that's taped and shown on national television each December. I told him I would love to, but needed him to clear it with NPR. He did, and each year since, I've had the good fortune of being the show's announcer.

Honors is the highlight of the Washington cultural year and is held at the Kennedy Center Opera House. If you've been there or seen it on television, you know it is a swanky event featuring the biggest names in the entertainment world. I've introduced dozens of people over the years, including Morgan Freeman, Barbra Streisand, Mel Brooks, Bruce Springsteen, Robert DeNiro, Twyla Tharp, Paul McCartney, Pete Townshend and Roger Daltrey of The Who, Meryl Streep, Neil Diamond, Yo-Yo Ma, Led Zeppelin, David Letterman, Shirley MacLaine, Billy Joel, Carlos Santana, and many others. The President and First Lady are typically there, and it is such a thrill to say the words, "Ladies and gentlemen, the President of the United States and Mrs. Michelle Obama."

It's a glamorous, prestigious event. The ladies are dazzling in their evening gowns and we men are in our tuxedos. I drop by the "green room" and introduce myself to the honored guests, then

<u>PRESIDENTIAL PARTY
ENTRANCE</u>

ANNOUNCER (VO-ATPB)
Ladies and Gentlemen, the Secretary of State
and Mrs. Teresa Heinz Kerry.
     [TEH'RAY-SA]

Ladies and gentlemen, the President of the
United States and Mrs. Michelle Obama.

ANNOUNCER (VO-ATPB)
Ladies and Gentlemen, please remain standing
for our "National Anthem".

Ladies and gentlemen, a 2013 recipient of the
Presidential Medal of Freedom, Arturo Sandoval.

BUDDY GUY
DUSTIN HOFFMAN
DAVID LETTERMAN
NATALIA MAKAROVA
LED ZEPPELIN

Produced by:
GEORGE STEVENS, JR.
Produced by:
MICHAEL STEVENS
Directed by:
LOUIS J. HORVITZ

KENNEDY
CENTER
HONORS

2012

John F. Kennedy Center for the Performing Arts
VTR: Sunday, December 2, 2012
AIR: CBS • Wednesday, December 26, 2012 • 9p EST

walk to a far corner in the back of the huge Opera House stage where I sit, all alone, in a tiny, storage closet-like room. I have my scripts, a TV monitor to see what is going on, and a headset to hear cues from the directors who are sitting in a studio truck outside.

After the show, there's always a black tie dinner in the atrium of the Kennedy Center. Tables are spread throughout the beautiful lobby and you're given a table number. And then you sit down to enjoy a wonderful evening meal with fascinating people. What a grand evening!

I asked Michael Stevens to add a few words, but before he does, allow me to tell you about Michael and his father, George Stevens, Jr., who are the ultimate pros. I have learned so much from working with them. They are part of entertainment royalty, with each of them winning multiple Emmy awards for producing, directing and writing. George, Jr.'s production of *The Thin Red Line* was nominated for several Oscars, and he was founder of the American Film Institute, where he produced programs saluting the biggest stars of the 20th century. His father, George Stevens, was an Oscar-winning director, and older generations of the Stevens family were also in acting and directing. Here's Michael:

Waking up to the words coming from my radio, "From NPR News in Washington, I'm Carl Kasell," resonated with me in terms of their simplicity. There was a clarity and truth to them with no need to sell, no need to manipulate. We have always liked the idea on our productions that the announcer does just that; that he or she is not shilling or trying to rev up the audience. Rather, it's a simple, declaratory statement of who is coming out on stage.

It goes back to the traditional "voice of God" approach,

but what's nice about Carl's voice is that it's not thunderous, there's a certain lilt to it, and he always gives a little inflection depending on who is coming on stage. He has become the best announcer we've ever had at the Kennedy Center Honors.

We tape Honors *on the first Sunday in December, and in 2013, because of Carl's* Wait Wait...Don't Tell Me! *travel schedule, he wasn't sure he could be with us for the whole weekend. So we took a sound man to his house and recorded his announcements. Because Carl is such a pro and knows the show so well, we really couldn't tell a difference.*

For close to the past ten years, we've been proud to have Carl as part of our Kennedy Center Honors *family.*

It's been a privilege to be the announcer for *Honors*, and I look forward to continuing.

north carolina

Here's to the land of the Long Leaf Pine,
The summer land where the sun doth shine,
Where the weak grow strong and the strong grow great,
Here's to North Carolina, the good old Tar Heel state.

— Author unknown. Printed on a postcard circa 1865.
North Carolina Collection, UNC at Chapel Hill Library

Being a Tar Heel means more to me than just rooting for the UNC sports teams. I love my home state, and even though I moved away in 1965, my heart has always been there. I never miss a chance to spread the word about its wonderfulness, including tips on where to find the best barbecue. I love going back for visits.

In July of 2014, Mary Ann and I attended a retirement party thrown for me by WUNC, and I had the opportunity to meet many listeners, including a young couple: Faith Klein and Howie Sanborn. They have quite a story. Howie served two years in Iraq as an Army Airborne Ranger, a member of the elite Golden Knights paratrooper unit. A marathoner and triathlete, Howie met Faith at a triathlon in 2012. Six months later, Howie was on a bike ride in Missouri when he was hit from behind by a vehicle. The accident broke his neck and severed his spinal cord, paralyzing him from the waist down.

I was told that "surrender is not in Howie's vocabulary" and after many surgeries and rehab, he resumed competing in triathlons. As he crossed the finish line at a wheelchair road race in March of 2014, Faith took his hand and proposed to him. Here's more from reporter Carol Jackson's account on the WUNC.org website.

> *"She stole my thunder," Howie said. "We're competi-tive." Howie felt that he had to outdo Faith's proposal. And then, he thought of legendary NPR announcer Carl Kasell. He'd heard on the radio that Kasell was coming to town for a retirement party hosted by WUNC.*
>
> *"We both love WUNC and NPR. I thought that I had missed the opportunity [to attend the Carl Kasell event.] But then I heard on the radio there were still tickets, so I called in."*
>
> *Howie's plan was just to get Carl to autograph the ring box. Instead, Carl Kasell used that recognizable voice to as-sist in the proposal. Kasell quieted the crowd and told Faith that Howie had a question to ask her. The memory of that moment will last a lifetime, Faith said.*

Photos by Carol Jackson, WUNC.org

Facilitating the proposal   *The ring box with my autograph*

226

Speaking of WUNC, I asked my longtime friend there, Regina Yeager, the director of development, to add a few thoughts.

I've worked at WUNC for over 22 years. I interviewed Carl during my first couple of years here and ended my story with the following statement: "Carl Kasell, proof positive that nice guys don't finish last." He's such a great guy and one of the nicest people I've ever met. Jokingly I've asked him if he could adopt me.

We had become good friends, and he would visit here often. He's a Tar Heel fan through and through and would come to watch the football and basketball games. When I told him I was getting married, he kept asking me to send him an invitation to the wedding. And I thought, that's sweet; he probably wants to send me a gift.

But as I came down the aisle after marrying my husband, there was Carl. He had flown to Louisiana for my wedding! I have a picture of me (in my wedding dress) and Carl displayed in my office and people will often ask, "Is that your dad?" "No," I say, "that's Carl Kasell!" Carl gave me the sweetest gift. My wedding was about a year after his mother and his wife, Clara, had passed away. Clara liked to paint pottery, and he gave me one of the pottery plates that had been hanging in their kitchen. Carl said he hoped I would have as many great meals as Clara and he did.

When Carl met Mary Ann, he started bringing her to sports events at UNC. One day we were in the stands at a UNC-Duke football game and it was late in the game. Mary Ann looked at him and said, "Carl, I'm ready to go. Could we go to the Botanical Garden?" And Carl said, "Oh, sure, Mary Ann." Carl left a Tar Heel game? I knew they were in love and destined to get married after that!

The thing about Carl is that as much as fans love him, he is even more beloved inside public radio. Everybody who's ever worked with him, every station he's ever visited, loves him. He is so appreciative of the employees at the stations, listeners and donors, and all the efforts necessary to make public radio possible. He stops to talk and listen to people and he thanks them, over and over. Carl is just a genuinely nice guy.

howard stern

In 2010, when Howard Stern heard that he was in the running to be inducted into the National Radio Hall of Fame, and that he was up against me for the honor, he talked about it on his satellite radio show:

Stern: *"Who is Carl Kuh-SELL?"*

Unknown male voice: *"He's on National Public Radio."*

Stern: *"Ooh! What a career! You're kidding? He got himself all the way to National Public Radio? What a lucky duck. Wow. Give it to him! He's way more successful in this business than me. He's gotta be, he's on NPR! Isn't that a national terrestrial thing?"*

Being nominated to the National Radio Hall of Fame was a magnificent honor, and I will always be grateful to my longtime friend and radio programming pioneer, Jim Russell, for nominating me, and to Bob Edwards for inducting me. I recorded a video reply to Stern:

"My dear Mr. Stein; I wrote this response because I wanted to be sure that I said the right things. My under-

standing is that you're featured on a satellite information service available in some brands of cars on which you host a show about gynecology. While I am sure this is a useful service for medical professionals, like all of us in radio you aspire to something greater. Best of luck to you."

NPR friends attending my 2010 National Radio Hall of Fame induction in Chicago included Jean Cochran and Bob Edwards. The honor was made even sweeter because so many of the radio heroes from my boyhood are in the Hall.

(Editors' note: Howard Stern was chosen for induction into the National Radio Hall of Fame in 2012. He did not attend the ceremony.)

so long, suckers!

Jerry A. Schulman

May 8, 2014

Carl: *From NPR and WBEZ, Chicago, this is* Wait Wait...Don't Tell Me!, *the NPR news quiz. I'm Carl Kasell and here's your host at the Chase Bank Auditorium in downtown Chicago, Peeeeeeter Sagal!*

(loud applause)

Peter: *Thanks everybody. We have a great show today ... but first, as many of you have already heard, Carl Kasell has an announcement to make*

Carl: *So long, suckers!*

(loud laughter and applause)

Peter: *That's right, after 60 years in broadcasting, including more than 30 years at NPR and this show's official judge and scorekeeper from the very first episode, Carl has decided to lay down the microphone and become our Scorekeeper Emeritus. He will continue to record voice mails for all our winners. He'll hang around our offices and he'll make sure we don't lower our standards.*

Carl: *As if that is even possible.*

(loud laughter and applause)

Peter: *He'll be with us for a few more months, at least. We now begin with our Carl Kasell Farewell Tour. In the meantime, we'll wring every last ounce of dignity from him.*

"Hi everybody, this is Barack from Washington. Carl, for 30 years on *Morning Edition,* yours was the voice that America woke up to. You brought us news of everything from presidential elections to the fall of the Berlin Wall. We trusted you to tell us what happened and why it mattered.

And then, for some reason, you joined a show where Peter Sagal makes you read goofy limericks and imitate everyone from Britney Spears to Barack Obama. It turns out they all sound like Carl Kasell. Anyway, we're glad you did it. Over the years, *Wait Wait...Don't Tell Me!* has become an institution in my hometown of Chicago and across the country. And Carl, you've been its heart and soul. I will never forget my time on the show. A lot of people didn't know my name but you guys were already making fun of it. Carl, congratulations on an incredible career and a well-deserved retirement. We will miss you, but it's good to know that you won't be giving up everything. Who knows? Maybe in a few years you'll get a call from another contestant: Barack from Chicago, and if I win, I'm glad you will still record my voice mail."

From Carl's final show, May 17, 2014

233

Congratulations, Carl. Stephen Colbert here, just saying what everyone else is thinking: all of us who loved you on NPR; all of us who listened for your voice every week on *Wait Wait* are so, so sad, sad that you're going to go, go.

Best of luck. Send us some limericks, or something. Very few things rhyme with Carl, by the way. I tried. The rhyming dictionary goes, "Carl, gnarl and snarl." Then it goes in to bull**** like "curl" and "seed pearl." You were dealt a rough hand when it came to a first name, I've gotta say. How ironic! Is that what irony means?

From Carl's final show, May 17, 2014

Stephen Colbert

To Carl,
With love and gratitude + best wishes for some serious R & R
Katie

I met Carl Kasell when I was an intern at WAVA All News Radio in Washington, DC, the summer after my freshman year in college. And I'll never forget how kind, encouraging, and generous he was. When I became interested in journalism, a lot of people weren't that enthusiastic, but I remember Carl always encouraged me to try to do my best and work hard in the business. He seemed to think that I actually had a future! Carl, thank you for giving a college student with big dreams her start. And thank you for being such a good person. I only hope by the time I retire, I'll have conducted my professional life with as much kindness, grace, humor and integrity as you have. Thank you again for everything. Good luck, Carl!

Katie Couric, 2014

acknowledgments

This book would not have happened without the guidance of my "agent," Mary Ann Foster. My publishers, Diane Montiel and Steve Alexander at Bantry Bay Publishing in Chicago, were kind, thorough and efficient as they expertly assembled the memories of my life. I am grateful for the sharp eyes of copy editors and proofreaders Lindsay Eanet and Lisa Couch, and for the photo design assistance from Erica Lebsack.

With appreciation and love, I thank the following:

Joe, Lynne, Kathleen, and Katiann Kasell
Brian, Csilla, Rocco, and Lydia Foster
Jackie Kasell • Mary Kasell Groce • Dr. William Gibson
Christopher Lawson, Wayne County Museum, Goldsboro, NC
Jack Kannan, Wayne Community College, Goldsboro, NC
The University of North Carolina at Chapel Hill • WUNC-FM
Mela Lawrence • Regina Yeager • Carol Jackson • Nina Graybill
Murray Horwitz • Jim Russell • Barry Gordemer • Bob Edwards
Susan Stamberg • Cokie Roberts • Nina Totenberg • Jean Cochran
Jay Kernis • Eric Nuzum • Anna Sebok • Margaret Low Smith
Doug Berman • Peter Sagal • Roxanne Roberts • Amy Dickinson
Adam Felber • Faith Salie • Paula Poundstone • Roy Blount, Jr.
Mike Danforth • Brian Babylon • Ian Chillag • Emily Ecton • Tom
Bodett • Mo Rocca • Diane Rehm • Eva Wolchover • Peter Jablow
Bill Buzenberg • Art Silverman • *Kennedy Center Honors:* George
Stevens, Jr. • Michael Stevens • Jerry A. Schulman • Melody Kramer
Debra Kirsch • Barbara Sopato • Jenna Meade • Janice Galvan • John
Burke, and so many others who have enriched my life.

a listener's limericks for carl

There once was this cat named Carl Kasell,
Who became some kind of NPR vassal.
He is the Tom Brady-O,
Of NPR radio,
And'll always be King of that castle.

• • • • •

His delivery was always so facile,
Despite dealing with Peter's hassle.
One could only adore,
The way he kept score.
We'll miss you Carl Kasell!

From Wait Wait *fan Jim Morrison, a reporter for the Newton TAB in Massachusetts*